Finding Elijah

FOLLOWING HIS FOOTSTEPS IN CIVIL WAR VIRGINIA

Geneva G. Lindner, M.A., M.Ed.

www.mascotbooks.com

Finding Elijah: Following his Footsteps in Civil War Virginia

For more information, please contact:
Mascot Books
560 Herndon Parkway #120
Herndon, VA 20170
info@mascotbooks.com

Library of Congress Control Number: 2016909913

CPSIA Code: PBANG0916A
ISBN-13: 978-1-63177-839-1

Printed in the United States

I dedicate this book to my beloved family:
Danny, Eric, and Alex.

I extend my heartfelt gratitude to all of you for your encouragement and support along this very interesting journey of finding Elijah. I am very grateful to all of you for humoring me, patiently listening to my stories both around the dinner table and on those much-loved long car rides to all those great family adventures we had.

To Eric Lindner, my dear first son, who encouraged me, visited cemeteries with me, participated in reenactments with me, and loves the Civil War.

To Alex Lindner Zorychta, my dear second son, to whom I will be forever indebted to for his outstanding editing; his continuous, unwavering positive attitude; and his constant encouragement throughout the entire process on this long-awaited endeavor.

To Dan Lindner, my dear husband and outstanding navigator, who accompanied me on all my adventures to find Elijah—stopping at every historical Civil War sign along the country roads, enduring being stuck in the mud, and sharing his in-depth knowledge of Civil War battles.

I am blessed to have all of you in my life, and I love you dearly. Without you, Elijah may have never been found!

Elijah F. Hutchison
(16 January 1826–13 January 1902)

Married 18 September 1845 to Susan Ann Harden

CONTENTS

CHAPTER 1:
The Journey Begins

I'm told that fate always intervenes; somehow, life's journey has brought me from the secluded comfort of those cherished childhood stories to living in the land where those stories originated. The journey to my ancestral land seems uncanny; and moreover, I never could have predicted that I would be looking for my great-great-grandfather, Elijah Franklin Hutchison, with such a profound passion. As it happened, soon after I was honorably discharged from the U.S. Navy, we packed up and moved from the beautiful sunny beaches of San Diego, California, to the oldest English colony in America: Virginia. It was June of 1985. Coincidentally, we settled very near the ancestral lands where Elijah was born on the cold winter's day of 18 January 1826 on the Hutchison Homestead, built 1732 in Chantilly, Virginia. What are the odds that I was to build a life here? I'm guessing that it truly was fate, and my great adventure to find Elijah has been an extraordinary one.

From the earliest time I can remember first comprehending just how magnificent these stories were, I loved to hear my Grandma Geneva (along with Aunt Florence) share the excitement of those bygone days about her Grandfather Elijah. She believed he lived on a plantation in Virginia, and she spoke about his Civil War soldier days, his fourteen children, and their perfect lives on their plantation. Wow, a Civil War soldier! Beautiful ladies in their Southern gowns with hoopskirts! A beloved "mammy" who fed the children! Playing on a huge tree swing over the river! Collecting rainwater! Oh, how the dome of the U.S. Capitol Building shone in the sunshine! For a nine-year-old growing up in central Illinois, these beautifully shared memories of my great-grandfather, Rodney Harmon Hutchison, and his father, Elijah Franklin Hutchison, were a lifetime away.

Grandma Geneva

Of course, much to my disappointment, after a great deal of research I now know that these oral histories contained a great deal of embellishments, as well as a few truths. Here's an example:

> *"I will always remember his grin, twinkling blue eyes, and thin brown white hair, which wasn't completely gray, even when he died at eighty-seven years old. I don't ever remember him being mad, as he did not have a temper. That was Grandmother Emma—she ruled the roost with her temper. My mother, too, could be very difficult and blameful. Grandpa Rodney was so mild-mannered and happy. Grandpa was a warm, genuine person and seemed to love life to its fullest with his wonderful sense of humor."*

> -Memories of Shirley Marshall Holmes

It was sometime in the later years of the 1880's when Great-Grandpa Rodney and his next older brother, John, packed up and moved to Sangamon County, Illinois. They decided on that location because the state was affectionately called the Land of Lincoln, as President Abraham Lincoln lived and worked in the capital city of Springfield, located in Sangamon County, Illinois. Apparently, the boys chose Illinois because their father Elijah, a Confederate soldier, strongly disliked President Lincoln; he blamed the President for the horrors of the Civil War. Neither John nor Elijah had a great relationship with their father, perhaps because they were born after Elijah returned from the war. Aunt Florence used to share Rodney's story about the time Elijah threw him off the roof of their two-story house while they were repairing the roof. Apparently Elijah was upset with Rodney because he wasn't doing a careful job of nailing on the roofing.

I had always heard about the grandeur and how the first Hutchisons came from the old country of England and Scotland, and called themselves Scotch-Irish. The stories literally spellbound us. They had been wonderfully told to us as young ones since we could remember by my mother and my aunts, especially my very favorite aunt, Aunt Florence, and grandmother Geneva. How did they collect all of these wonderful histories, having lived in the heart of the Illinois prairieland their entire lives?

The father of Grandma Geneva Susie Hutchison Wilham, Rodney Harmon Hutchison, was born in June 1866 at the old family home in Western Fairfax County, Virginia, in the rolling hills of the Old Dominion countryside on the Virginia Piedmont. He was the last of fourteen children to be brought into the world by Elijah Franklin and Susan Ann Hardin (Harden or Harding) Hutchison. His twin, Rose, sadly died within her first few months of life—supposedly because there was not enough mother's milk for her to drink. Grandmother had spoken about a beloved "Mammy," who tended the children, but I have found no evidence of any slaves owned by Susan and Elijah—this was immediately after the war ended in 1865, and like most Virginia farm families, they were destitute. The land was in a ruinous condition, and they had no money. Times were difficult. In addition, Elijah had a love for the firewater and had difficulty staying sober. He owed quite a lot of money to one of his relatives, Silas Hutchison, and his Uncle Lucien Fitzhugh. The land Elijah's family lived on had been passed down in the Hutchison family, but sadly had to be parceled off and sold, including the land which, in the present day, is part of Washington International Dulles Airport. Just an interesting aside, Dulles Airport was named after President Dwight D. Eisenhower's Secretary of State, and is located in both Fairfax and Loudoun Counties in Virginia—a site personally chosen by President Eisenhower.

My curiosities were inspired with every family dinner we had with Aunt Florence and Grandma Geneva. They said I asked so many questions that I was just like a talking doll. Back then, one of the most-loved dolls was called Chatty Kathy, so of course, they nicknamed me "Chatty" Jennie. I didn't mind. First off, I loved my dolly, and second, I wanted to know more about the olden days. So, when I was in high school, I began to bring a notebook anytime my parents planned a trip from our home just outside of Peoria, Illinois to Jerseyville, Illinois. I loved these road trips; there was always a great deal of anticipation, and we counted the days until our departure. When the day finally

My family, 1968, with whom I had many adventures to Jerseyville, Illinois. Left to right: Ann (Mom), Geneva "Jennie", Matthew, and Paul (Dad). Photographer unknown

arrived, we always arose early in the morning and anxiously packed up the car with blankets, small suitcases, pillows, and snacks, as well as Dixie cups for nice cold water from our thermos, which my mother so lovingly filled with ice and water. About three times a year, we would made the 175-mile journey along the narrow Illinois roads and over the old bridges along and through the flat prairie farmland to Jerseyville. I didn't even mind the carsickness that I always had, because I was going to see my favorite people. I would simply lie down on my half of the back seat and listen to the mesmerizing clickity-clack sound of the tires as we sped along the old roads.

We always stopped at the Old Route 66 Ariston Café in Litchfield, Illinois for a rest, a snack, and some gas. Mom and Dad would have coffee with cream and sugar and my dad, oh

1974. Aunt Florence and Uncle Willard
Photographer unknown

Jerseyville, Illinois, our best family gatherings. 1973.
Left to right: Florence Wilham Moeller, Pauline Wilham Ander
Geneva Hutchison Wilham, Maxine Wilham Nohl, Betty Wil
Prunty, Ann Wilham Astel. Photographer unknown

he just loved pie—any kind of pie—so they would each have a piece of pie. My brother and I would usually get some ice cream; chocolate, if you please.

Our arrival was just as much anticipated by Aunt Florence, Uncle Willard, and their teenage children Darlene ("Gay"), Sue, and Don. Remember, this was the era when there were no cell phones and people watched the clock. As we drove up their gravel driveway, out came Grandma Geneva, Aunt Florence, and Uncle Willard. Aunt Florence would hug us so tightly I thought I was going to burst; and, of course, Grandma always pinched our cheeks and kissed us with her bright red lipstick (and yes, we had that lip imprint on our cheeks for hours!). She loved her bright red lipstick. Yuck! And the smell of her perfume, Chantilly, was left behind on our clothes.

Everything was much abuzz as everyone helped finish the last part of dinner, which always happened at noon with the idea that everyone could eat yummy leftovers as we told stories. Dinner was always a lively affair at Aunt Florence's house: everyone excitedly talking and telling stories about the other relatives who were not there, or sharing the letters they had received—back in the day, the five sisters (my mother Ann and her sisters Betty, Maxine, Pauline, and Florence) would write letters back and forth on a weekly basis, sometimes even more often. (Needless to say, reading and sharing the old letters was a treat for us.) Cousin Krista Kell, Gay Moeller's daughter, has been the guardian of most of these greatly treasured letters. What news was there about Aunt Pauline in Huron, Ohio, or news of Aunt Maxine of Goodfield, Illinois, or Aunt Betty in Metamora, Illinois? A long-distance telephone call was very expensive, so the sisters wrote many letters during this time.

Uncle Willard had a magical garden in which he grew the world's best green beans, tomatoes, lettuce, carrots, and his sweet Illinois corn. As we all sat down to a wonderful smorgasbord of healthy, tasty food, Uncle Willard blessed our meal, which had been so lovingly prepared by Aunt Florence. Even as the smell of the sweet macaroni cheese and cornbread wafted across the table, Uncle Willard began:

Come Lord Jesus
Be our Guest
Let these gifts
To us be blessed.

The much-loved meal was prepared by Aunt Florence with Uncle Willard's latest garden harvests, which thankfully included her world famous creamy homemade macaroni and cheese baked casserole. There was so much talking, visiting, and wonderful foods, that everyone was very full. After dinner, we sat around the old kitchen table on vinyl-covered chairs from the 1940's. We listened with excitement to yet another great story of our ancestors, while eating yummy chocolate cream pie, lemon pie, or cherry pie, along with a much-coveted glass of ice-cold milk, or "sodie pop" with ice, poured in the old aluminum drinkware. There was never just one pie, because Auntie was deathly afraid someone would be hungry.

As we began dessert, the same conversation about our Hutchison ancestors and Elijah always came up, the truth often embellished after being told over and over again. And there would always be new remembrances I was able to write down on my notepad. What I am about to share with you are the results of many long hours spent, years later, on finding the truth about my beloved Elijah, who seems to have always been a part of me with his sense of adventure and zest for life.

CHAPTER 2:
Elijah Franklin Arrives

On 16 January 1826, a healthy baby boy, Elijah Franklin Hutchison, Jr., entered into antebellum Virginia, a world of a slave-based agriculture and strongly held Southern traditions. Born to Elijah Hutchison, Sr., and his mistress, "Mary Erton," the little boy would be raised by his father and his father's legal wife, Sarah Harrison Fitzhugh (1802–1866). This particular year, 1826, was a watershed year in American history, for July 4 would remain forever embedded in American minds, as the 50th Anniversary remembrances of the Revolutionary War for Independence gave reason for a much-celebrated holiday. The anniversary celebrated the day when Thomas Jefferson, a Virginian, penned the infamous letter of Rights and Grievances to King George III of Great Britain that history named the Declaration of Independence.

In reflecting on the real reason why I decided to pursue Elijah's journey, I realized that it stemmed from a desire to connect with my family's past. We are all a product of our past. After I arrived in Virginia and began collecting basic research, I was disappointed to learn that important records such as birth records, land records, wills, and other vital documents had been burned during the Civil War. I had many questions about the

The Hutchison House, Western Fairfax, Virginia. Photo by G. Lindner

people who raised Elijah: his father and step-mother, Elijah, Sr. and Sarah Fitzhugh, namely their life together, but I was searching for personal information from the 1830's and had nowhere to find these answers. I have been unable to find any diaries, social column news, or other Hutchison family primary source records with the degree of detail I desired. How did they meet? Was this an arranged marriage? What did they have in common? The difficult reality for me throughout this pilgrimage has been accepting the fact that such miniscule details are lost to history that we shall never know.

Sarah brought to the marriage her social status, which placed her husband and children in the gentry class—the highest socio-economic class in antebellum Virginia. Louisa Skinner Hutchison, a well-known and well-respected genealogist of Loudoun County, Virginia, located official documentation on Elijah Franklin Hutchison, Jr., regarding his birth status: "Regrettably, he is declared a 'bastard' within his county records," Louisa explained. During this time period, regardless of whether both parents were well-respected, these children remained labeled throughout their lives and were scorned.

Many of baby Elijah Franklin's uncles also married women of this class, and as a result, this Hutchison lineage is now entwined with many of Virginia's founding fathers. As Lori Hutchison Maxwell, a descendant of John Lewis Hutchison (Rodney's older brother), and I began in-depth research into our Hutchison family, we found family linkages to the Lees, the Washingtons, the Harrisons, and the Fitzhughs. How exciting it was to learn that we are related to the pioneers, who came and settled this wild Virginia land that was named after the virgin Queen Elizabeth I.

Less than six months after baby Elijah Franklin first tasted the bounties of homegrown fare and learned how to crawl, two of America's beloved founding fathers would pass to the next world. Thomas Jefferson passed first, at eighty-two years old, five hours before John Adams did at ninety years old. After they had battled the injustices together with pens in hand, they had many years of personal turmoil in their friendship—some good, and many bad—over political differences.

> *Life's visions are vanished, its dreams are no more.*
> *Dear friends of my bosom, why bathed in tears?*
> *I go to my fathers; I welcome the shore,*
> *which crowns all my hopes, or which buries my cares.*
> *Then farewell my dear, my lov'd daughter, Adieu!*
> *The last pang of life is in parting from you!*
> *Two Seraphs await me, long shrouded in death:*
> *I will bear them your love on my last parting breath.*
> *A death-bed Adieu. Th: J. to MR.*[1]

As I began to search and find those places where my Elijah left his footprint of life, I found that in the 1830 census, Elijah was living with his father and Sarah, his father's wife. Five years later, his sister, Elizabeth ("Lizzy") entered this world. He loved her very much, and they shared the same birth mother. His very loving stepmother, Sarah, raised him as a child of her gentry society, and as such, there were certain expectations already set for him.

Throughout his adolescent years, Elijah was privileged, and attended the numerous social events required of the upper class with his stepmother and father. He would have been taught the attributes of a gentleman, which included horsemanship, dancing, impeccable manners, and schooling in the necessary matters of business. These skills, especially his horsemanship skills, would serve him well throughout his life.

As Elijah grew up, Virginians fell upon hard times and he saw many folks' economic situations change from what was normal to difficult. The Financial Panic of 1837 had devastated many Virginia families because President Andrew Jackson did not re-charter the National Bank, and modified the law to demand all payment in specie. Needless to say, the situation trickled down: land prices were depressed, farmers lost a lot of money, and overall the economy was in a sad state. People packed up their Conestoga wagons and headed west, along the Great Wagon Road, through the Shenandoah Gap or Cumberland Gap into Ohio or Kentucky, where land was much cheaper. Times were changing, and the government was not equipped or inclined to assist people during those days. Today, we have the Federal Reserve, created in 1914 during President Wilson's term, whose job is to help regulate our free market economy.

Records show that some of the Hutchison clan took advantage of this economic opportunity, and a part of the group ended up in Kansas and even as far as California.

These hardships did not pass over Elijah Sr. and his loving family. According to Lori Hutchison Maxwell's family research, around 1838, when Elijah, Jr. was eleven years old, he became aware of the dire financial situation of his parents. Elijah, Sr. was in debt. He had a twin brother, Ely, and the brothers seemed to be very close. When Elijah, Sr. fell on these difficult times, Ely and his son, Silas, held his property in various trusts. Silas and Elijah, Jr. remained close throughout their lives. Young Elijah was also close to another cousin, William Alexander Hutchison, and it appears as though William was Elijah, Jr.'s only loyal relative throughout the years. Moreover, Lucien Fitzhugh, Sarah's brother, helped ensure that Elijah, Jr. and his sister Elizabeth were both well cared for. He did not have a close relationship with his other cousins from the Lee, Fitzhugh, Wren, or Cross families. Ultimately, Elijah, Sr. turned over all of his holdings held in trust except for the Dranesville store and ordinary,

Dranesville property: To the best of our knowledge, this is the Tavern and Ordinary where Elijah, Sr., and Susan were innkeepers. Photo by G. Lindner

located in western Fairfax County, Virginia, which he held onto.

When I visited the very charming Dranesville Ordinary, it was a beautiful, bright crisp Virginia spring day. As I stood on the hill, I closed my eyes and I was taken back to simpler times. I could see our young Elijah riding his horse around the rolling hills. and Sarah ringing the bell to call him home for dinner. I was very pleased to know that instead of tearing down this beautiful ordinary, it had been moved about 125 feet to make way for the new, widened Route 7. Throughout the years, this well-situated ordinary provided an invaluable service to weary travelers making their way to the Great Wagon Road. These travelers stopped and rested before continuing their journey to find what they felt would be a better way of life for their families. Rooms for the night were sold by the space in the bed, most often with five spaces to a bed. I'm very grateful to Fairfax County Park Authority for saving this beloved building.

Remember your teenage years, and the difficulties you faced on determining your path to adulthood? During this time period, children really did not have much choice on their path to adulthood; rather, it was dictated by parental decision. There must have been much consternation and discussion as the family tried to decide the course that Elijah, Jr.'s career would take him. The discussion ended in the decision to send Elijah away to be a carpenter's apprentice. It is heartbreaking to imagine the sadness and hurt that he must have felt as he left the only home he had ever experienced to begin anew as a carpenter's apprentice in Leesburg, Virginia.

Officially incorporated in 1813 and named to honor Thomas Lee, who was Robert E. Lee's great-grand-uncle, this town was a major stopping point for travelers, who traveled the small two-lane Old Carolina Road (modern-day Route 15), from North to South. Leesburg is located in Loudoun County, Virginia, not far from where Elijah was born. As a matter of fact, Elijah would later ride this road during the beginning of the Civil War with his 6th Virginia Cavalry. As I began to try to find these places from the twenty-first century, it would have been very helpful to me if I only had an old map overlay (perhaps that is my next project!). As I drove around Dranesville on that crisp spring day, there were no other old houses that had been preserved other than the ordinary that had been operated by Elijah, Sr., then Sarah, and finally Elijah, Jr.

During Elijah's adolescent years in Leesburg, Virginia, there were numerous slaves, many of who were quite talented and skilled artisans. It is rumored that Elijah, Jr.'s great uncle, Benjamin, owned slaves. Often, slave owners would "loan" out their slaves. Interestingly, at this point in time, I can find no personal connection with Hutchison friends in town, which leads me to the conclusion that Elijah, Sr. had business dealings with a Leesburg, Virginia businessman, James Stafford, who was to be young Elijah's apprentice. Unfortunately for our young Elijah, because he was a "bastard" child he had to leave the comfort of his Hutchison/Fitzhugh clan and relocate to Leesburg, Virginia. This type of class discrimination in antebellum Virginia was very real, despite the fact that his gentry class stepmother, Sarah Harrison Fitzhugh Hutchison, loved him very much and always demonstrated her support for him.

Thus began the next chapter in Elijah, Jr.'s life. Now, he was officially an apprentice carpenter, bound to James Stafford of Leesburg, Virginia until he came of age. Mr. Stafford taught Elijah the skills of a master carpenter, providing room, board, and some broader education in return for his labor. During the time he was "bound" to James Stafford, he wrote his official name as "Elijah Urton"—his birth mother's surname. According to Lori Maxwell Hutchison, "We are not sure why the county named him Elijah Erton; was it because the Hutchison's were so prominent in both Fairfax and Loudoun counties? Or was it a way to save the man's reputation? A woman is ruined without marriage, but not always a man. Elijah Franklin Hutchison fought for his Hutchison name always. Before this, he never wrote his name as 'Erton' (which has also shown up in some records as 'Urton')—always 'Hutchison'. This arrangement was part of a program where poor white or "bastard" children worked to learn skills until they came of age." At some point, Elijah, Jr. changed his name spelling to "El'jah".

One has to wonder if Elijah played any part in the decision to enter into the apprenticeship. As a result of this dramatic change in his life, he developed a chip on his shoulder with a bad temper and a sometimes-disagreeable personality. However, as time passed, it appeared as though his love for carpentry grew; he seemed to have a natural talent. As a result, he became confident and throughout the rest of his life he listed his occupation as Carpenter.

Our Elijah grew into an extremely handsome, dashing young man (although I will tell you that, indeed, all of our fine young male Hutchison descendants are very handsome). Family members described Elijah as being slender and tall, at six feet, with piercing blue eyes. His son, Rodney Hutchison, reported his dad as being left-handed. His hair was a beautiful light-reddish sandy brown and full of waves and curls when it grew longer.

As his Scotch-Irish luck would have it, his dream of moving

home to Pleasant Valley,—a small area on the outskirts Fairfax, Virginia—came to fruition. While living in Leesburg during this time, he met and charmed the heart of a beautiful woman, Susan Ann Harding (Hardin, Harden) from Washington, D.C. Was it a chance encounter at a party, a blind date, or an arranged marriage? The planets were aligned perfectly for Susan and Elijah, and Elijah (nineteen years old) and Susan (nineteen years, seven months old) were married. All census records show that both he and Susan were literate, and both could read and write, which would be expected of a man of his birth class. Sadly, I have been unable to find her birth certificate, but I have her marriage certificate. On 18 September 1845, they entered into marital bliss in Washington, D.C., but chose to return to Loudoun County, Virginia, where Elijah's father and Sarah gave the couple a handsome sum of land on which to begin their life together. Susan bore many healthy children, ten of whom lived into adulthood.

I was very curious as to why they were married in Washington, D.C., as the distance between Leesburg, Virginia and Washington, D.C. is about fifty miles, straight east on Leesburg Pike. Elijah knew this road very well, as his father's place of business, the Dranesville Ordinary, was located along this road. While I was looking at some Loudoun County records, I noticed that one of Elijah's cousins, William Hutchison, attested as a witness for any couples who were bound in marriage at Loudoun County Courthouse. It seems that the Hutchisons had many political as well as business connections in both Washington, D.C. and Leesburg; perhaps one of them had introduced the couple.

As I had been told in the stories from my grandmother, the happy couple was blessed with twelve children, two of whom did not make it to adulthood.

Child	Birth	Married	Death
Mary G.	1846	No information	No information
Robert Henry	February 1847	Mary Jane McCarthy 11 July 1882	21 May 1931 Alexandria, VA
James	December 1849		18 July 1856
Sarah Jane	1852	(1) Kidwell (2) Isaiah Gooding 5 January 1873	11 May 1938
Elijah Profitt (Prophet)	24 July 1854	Sarah Anne Kidwell 9 December 1875	5 May 1933 Annandale, VA Kidney Failure
Margaret Elizabeth	June 1857	Charles Henry Johnson	1909
Virginia Fairfax Hutchison	22 November 1859	James Thecker Fearson 13 February 1880	23 July 1940 Arlington, VA Salivary Gland Cancer
Abraham Franklin	1860	Dorothea Muhlsausen 25 April 1894	23 September 1925 Washington, D.C.
Lucinda	1861	No information	No information
Elijah departs for war on 22 April 1861			
John Lewis	2 February 1865	Cora Lula	3 June 1938 Springfield, IL
Rodney Harmon	1 June 1866	Emma Althetta Scott 12 August 1890 Springfield, IL	29 January 1955 Pneumonia Mt. Pulaski, Illinois
Rose	16 June 1867	August 1867	Failure to thrive

**The information on the table was compiled using Birth, Marriage, Death, Pension and Census Records from Ancestry.com.

In 1846, shortly after they were married, Mary G. entered their lives, and next came Robert Henry in 1847. In December 1849, James was born, who would pass on 18 July 1856. As of this date, I have been unable to discover where he is buried, or what took his young life. In 1852, Sarah was born, with Elijah Profitt entering this world after her on 24 July 1854, followed by Margaret in June 1857, and Virginia Fairfax on 22 November 1859. Lucinda would make her arrival sometime in 1861. I am not sure when, but as Elijah Franklin left home in April to join the war, he was not around for her early years. On 2 February 1865, John Lewis arrived, followed on 1 June 1866 by Rodney Harmon (my great, great grandfather) and his twin Rose, who passed shortly after her birth.

Sadly, in December 1846, Elijah, Sr. passed on, and Sarah Harrison Fitzhugh Hutchison, his beautiful, devoted wife, continued on without him. She looked to her stepson, Elijah, Jr. to help her out, which he did. Their close relationship would continue throughout the rest of her life, as he loved her dearly. She left this Earth in 1866, after the Civil War. Perhaps she saw the last of Elijah's children to enter this world.

A few years before the war broke out, Elijah, Jr. moved his family to Virginia to work at the grain mill, which is validated in the 1860 census. Aunt Florence always thought this was interesting, and for some unknown reason, the fact that Elijah had worked the mill in Aldie was always a topic of discussion at the family gathering table. We know that at least one child was born in Aldie. About eight years ago I also found out that at the original family homestead of Elijah, Sr., had a mill on the property at Cub Run, known as the Cub Run Mill. As fate would have it, I was at the annual meeting of the Centreville

Historic society as a member of the Board of Directors when I discovered this. We actually had an event where our group walked to the old site of the Cub Run Mill with a Fairfax County Park Historian. It was a lovely site for a mill; however, like most wooden buildings, it had been gone for many years, with just a few rocks that marked the original foundation. Near the mill, there is now a grade school, called Cub Run. It was a beautiful walk, and as I was looking through the woods I could imagine the family working the mill on the millstream, grinding the grains and bagging up the flour.

The 1850's flew by rapidly for Elijah and Susan, as they were totally immersed in raising children and making ends meet on a monthly basis. By the time Elijah was thirty-four, he and Susan already had a full house and many children to nurture and care for. Politically, at this point in Elijah's life, there had been much turmoil throughout Loudoun County, Virginia over the issue of expansion of slavery. The political rift was widening, despite the attempted compromises passed by Congress, as the North and South disagreed over the role of states' rights.

In the South, the economic system was built upon indentured servants and slave labor culture due to the very labor-intense needs of the crops of tobacco, cotton, rice, and indigo. The institution was perpetuated by the invention of Eli Whitney's cotton gin, which allowed a much faster cleaning of the cotton and amplified the economic profits enabled by slavery. As would be expected, the production of cotton quadrupled during this time period in Virginia. This increase in production brought about an urgent need for more slaves, and throughout the South the land became known as the "Cotton Kingdom." Notably, there was money in slaves because even

Aldie Mill, Aldie, VA. Photo by G. Lindner

though slavery imports had been outlawed in 1808 by the Constitutional Convention, yet the law did not address "slave breeding." In Fairfax and Alexandria counties, "slave breeding" houses had been established in the 1840's, whereby the slave children were sold in local auction houses located in Dranesville, Centreville, and Alexandria. These children were given household tasks as early as two years old, and sent to work in the fields as early as eight. Originally, the entirety of colonial America used slaves; however, after the Revolutionary War, most of the Northern economy had developed into an industrial economy, building factories and using the enormous natural resources of the land. In the North, there were more family-sized farms, numerous forests, rivers, and small towns, which resulted in a larger population of landowners. However, it is important to note that when the War began, the border states of Missouri, Maryland, Delaware, and Kentucky used slave labor in their agricultural economy, but did not secede from the Union.

In Virginia, there were more slaves than white families in the antebellum period. According to the 1860 U.S. Federal Census Slave Schedules, Virginia had half a million slaves, and it was reported that this was the highest number of slaves in any Southern state at the time. When I looked at the 1860 census, I noticed that the census taker spelled his last name as "Huckeson" and he was listed as living with Susan, Mary, Profitt, and six-month-old baby James. Also in the 1860 U.S. Federal Census Slave Schedules, E Hutchison is listed as having three slaves in Aldie, Virginia: male, 36, black; female, 35, Mulatto; and female, 30, Mulatto. Could this be Elijah or his Uncle Ely Hutchison?

While Elijah and his family were preparing for the winter of 1860, there was much political talk and a great deal of worry about what the future would bring. It was very uncertain and everyone was tense. The states that were further in the South were vehemently opposed to the election of Abraham Lincoln in November of 1860, which proved to be the final straw for southern discontent over the state of the Union. Immediately following this uncertain Presidential Election, southern states with a cash economy began holding statewide conventions and local elections to vote yes or no on secession. On 14 January 1861, authorization from the Virginia General Assembly was passed to hold a convention to discuss secession. It was a very solemn time in Virginia, because even though President-Elect Lincoln promised he would not abolish slavery, people were very worried about their slave labor economy and states' rights.

What exactly were states' rights? In Virginia, states' rights gave state governments the right to govern their state, as they saw fit. During this time period, joining the South's side was more about being a Virginian than an American. Not everyone wanted to leave the Union or secede, especially in the northwestern part of the state.

In 1860, in what originally was the western part of Virginia (along the I-81 corridor and across the mountains all the way to the Mississippi), the economy was quite different than that of eastern Virginia. Since Virginia's early colonial roots, settlers in this very hilly, mountainous territory developed a living with subsistence farms, hunting, and fishing. Compared to the Eastern part of Virginia, the geography of the lands was vastly different. In Eastern Virginia, the lowlands and Piedmont offered many fertile, flatter lands, conducive to vast agricultural areas of cash crop success. In its early days, tobacco was the most successful crop, brought to Jamestown by John Rolfe, an English botanist. For decades, this crop was known as "Virginia Gold" and there was a huge economic opportunity for wealthier colonists. In addition, only landowners could vote, so a large landowner had much-coveted voting rights, which they did not have in England due to the primogeniture laws. Needless to say, the lands in Western Virginia drew a completely different population. In the early days of colonial Virginia, it was possible to come to the new world without any money with a sponsor, which was an indentured servant. An Indenture Contract would be signed for a commitment of four to seven years' labor, after which time the individual would receive fifty acres of land in the western part of Virginia. The indentures worked the land for the plantation owner and labor was plentiful before the English Civil War (1641–1650). The colonies received all their manufactured goods from England and its other colonies; and, as part of the Triangular Trades which had developed between the Americas, England, and the Gold Coast, the slave trade got its American roots in 1619 when the first cargo of Africans showed up in Jamestown. After the English Civil War was over, fewer people were leaving England, and thus the large pool of labor was drying up. With the crops planted and much money being made, the labor system turned to Africans, as the Portuguese and Dutch merchants brought more and more captured Africans to trade, from the gold coast of Africa. As time passed, the people of western Virginia decided they did not want to be part of the Confederate States of America; so, they petitioned Congress to become a state, drew up a new constitution, and joined the Union on 14 June 1863.

When the murmurings of war began, not everyone was in favor of secession, as there were differences in the economic and social ways of life. Often, family members disagreed on politics. When the war fever broke out, brothers joined different sides. In the South, there was a large group of Unionists in each state, which formed regiments and fought against the Confederacy. Every Southern state had raised a regiment of Unionists who believed that the Union must be held together at all costs. Everyone was very afraid of what the future would bring if Virginia seceded, and many still wanted peace to prevail. There were political urgings to have a meeting with the President to see if another compromise could be found to avoid bloodshed; however, President Lincoln would not discuss peace with what he considered to be rebels.[2]

So on 17 April 1861, a secret convention was held in Virginia and delegates voted 88-55 for passage of the Ordinance of Secession. Soon after the vote from the Virginia Assembly, a mass meeting, separate from the secret meetings, was conducted in Leesburg, where the secessionists outnumbered the Unionists.[3] An official vote was conducted in May and the result was 1,626 to 726 for secession. Was Elijah present for this vote? He answered the call of patriotism and volunteered to serve on 22 April 1861 just after the General Assembly vote was tallied.[4]

I was not surprised to read that on 22 April 1861, thirty-five-year-old Elijah answered the political call of duty and volunteered as a Confederate soldier in Company K of Loudoun's 6th Virginia Cavalry, leaving his wife with many children to care for. He followed in the path of his ancestors: his father had served in the War of 1812, and his grandfather served as a Civil Servant in the American Revolution. Elijah was a fine horseman, so joining the cavalry made perfect sense. His eldest son, Robert Henry, wanted to join up along with his father, but he was only fourteen years old, so he went along as a water boy.

CHAPTER 3:
An Emotional Political Climate

At this point in my story, I want to share the very emotional political climate of this great country during the antebellum period, as so many lives were impacted even in that time of very limited social media—pretty much just newspapers and word of mouth. I have often pondered why we are so enamored with this bloody conflict that happened a century and a half ago. I still don't truly understand why these issues could not have been solved by compromise of some type. Why would this nation fight such a bloody war, knowing that there would be so many fine young Americans killed and that so many families would lose their sons because of their ideologies? Despite knowing there had been a number of sectional issues between the North and the South after the War of 1812, my question is still not answered.

Yes, the expansion of slavery played a central role, but the causes of the war had been brewing since 1815, and some believe as far back as the American Revolution. Both sides had very different viewpoints on what "sovereignty" meant and the interpretation of the Constitution, which was and is the Supreme Law of our land. There is no doubt that each region had very different economic systems, so throughout the 1800's Congress had passed many protective tariffs, which economically hurt the South. Protective tariffs were a tax placed on imported goods—an economic tool of the Federal Government, used to protect the integrity of American-made goods. This extra tariff essentially raised the cost of imported goods dramatically for the South.

Industrialization impacted the North from the late 1700's on, as the climate and economic ways there were far better suited to manufacturing. Not surprisingly, the North had developed into an industrial society with large factories, large family farms, and mills. Each region had different social systems and cultures, dating back to the beginning of the country, when brave colonists made their way to the new world of Virginia in 1607. So when Congress passed laws looking after Northern industrial needs, these measures became unintentionally punitive to the South. Southerners paid excessive taxes because they had to import nearly everything. On top of this, there were numerous anti-slavery abolitionists from many different areas throughout the country who loudly voiced their opinions.

In response to slavery being allowed in the Territories, the Republican Party was officially founded on 20 March 1854 in Ripon, Wisconsin, on the foundation of a desire to eradicate chattel slavery. John C. Frémont ran as the first presidential candidate for the Republican Party in 1856 on a free-soil platform, but was unsuccessful. The presidents of the 1850's (which included Zachary Taylor, Millard Fillmore, Franklin Pierce, and James Buchanan) chose not to deal with the issue of the expansion of slavery, nor even try to eradicate this institution, because they felt that it was not part of their executive powers.

One of the most prolific speeches of American history was

presented during these difficult times, as the state of the Union went from bad to worse. Hysteria began to grip the South, as the 1860 election was fast approaching. On 16 June 1858, Abraham Lincoln, of Springfield, Illinois, gave one of his most famous speeches, based on Matthew 13:26, about the sad state of affairs in our country as his acceptance speech before over 1,000 Republican Delegates at the Illinois Republican State Convention His initial goal was to preserve the Union at all costs, and in Abraham Lincoln's famous house-divided speech, he very profoundly stated,

> "...In *my* opinion, it *will* not cease, until a *crisis* shall have been reached, and passed...A house divided against itself cannot stand...I believe this government cannot endure, permanently half *slave* and half *free*...I do not expect the Union to be *dissolved*—I do not expect the house to *fall*—but I *do* expect it will cease to be divided...It will become *all* one thing or *all* the other...Either the *opponents* of slavery, will arrest the further spread of it, and place it where the public mind shall rest in the belief that it is in the course of ultimate extinction; or its *advocates* will push it forward, till it shall become alike lawful in *all* the States, *old* as well as *new*—*North* as well as *South*..."

> [source emphasis]
> Abraham Lincoln, 16 June 1858,
> Springfield, Illinois

The Supreme Court had just rendered the 1857 Dred Scott Decision, Dred Scott v. Sandford, 60 U.S. 393, whereby the majority opinion held that slaves were property; therefore, the Court interpreted that it was unconstitutional for the Federal Government to pass laws prohibiting slavery in any American Territory. People were in shock at the outcome of the decision and felt this decision was a reversal of the democratic principles upon which our country was founded.

When our founding fathers were writing our Constitution in 1787, they used a great many of the English and French philosophical ideologies. One in particular that Thomas Jefferson greatly admired were those ideas of English philosopher John Locke (1632–1704), who believed all men had natural rights of life, liberty, and property that could not be denied to any man by virtue of birth. In composing the Bill of Rights to ensure the people would always be protected from any despotic government in 1790, James Madison adopted many of these basic ideas of liberty and democracy. Congress added these addendums or changes to the U.S. Constitution. For example, Amendment V states,

> "No person shall be held to answer for a capital, or otherwise infamous crime, unless on a presentment or indictment of a grand jury, except in cases arising in the land or naval forces, or in the militia, when in actual service in time of war or public danger; nor shall any person be subject for the same offense to be twice put in jeopardy of life or limb; nor shall be compelled in any criminal case to be a witness against himself, nor be deprived of life, liberty,

or property, without due process of law; nor shall private property be taken for public use, without just compensation."

United States Constitution, 1790

I now want to share a little background on the attempts to compromise that were made by our leaders; however, these compromises were unable to solve problems on any long-term basis. Politically, the country was in a terrible state, with the expansion of slavery the top issue of the day in Congress. In an effort to appease both factions, Henry Clay, also known as the Great Compromiser, came up with three different compromises during this antebellum period, which were passed in an attempt to keep slave and free states balanced in Congress for voting on legislation: the Missouri Compromise of 1820, the Compromise of 1850, and the Kansas-Nebraska Act of 1854.

The Missouri Compromise of 1820 stated that, while Missouri could come in as a slave state, Maine (which was the other part of land from the original colony of Massachusetts) would enter the Union as a free state. It also set a boundary of the 36°30' latitude line, above which no states would have slaves with the exception of slave states that were already intact, such as Kentucky, Virginia, Maryland, and Delaware.

Interestingly, when California came in as a free state with the Compromise of 1850, the Executive Branch promised to enforce the Fugitive Slave Act, which hired numerous U.S. Marshals and bounty hunters to hunt down any runaway slave and return them to the rightful owner. However, often these slave catchers were ruthless, kidnapping innocent free blacks and selling them into slavery. It was a very traumatic time for free blacks and runaway slaves. Some states had created personal liberty laws, while others turned a blind eye.

The third compromise was the Kansas-Nebraska Act of 1854, which promoted popular sovereignty. This encouraged a race to the Kansas-Nebraska Territory by both pro- and anti-slavery proponents, and whoever applied for statehood first would determine the status of slavery there. Emotions were running high and the Kansas area became known as Bloody Kansas, where America witnessed the first American terrorist, John Brown, whose plan for eradicating slavery was to kill all the slave owners in Kansas Territory using machetes. Free Soilers won this battle, creating a free territory by 1859. On 29 January 1861, Kansas would enter as a free state in the Union.

As election time was nearing, the Southerners were very much afraid they would be forced to end slavery. They believed that power should remain in the states if Abraham Lincoln was elected, because he was from Illinois and supported the Republican Party, which disavowed slavery. Lincoln repeatedly told the country that while he would not interfere with slaves, the Union would be preserved above all else. Abraham Lincoln was the second Republican candidate to run on the new Republican Party ticket. In 1860, presidential candidate Lincoln was not even on some Southern ballots. However, he won the Presidential Election by a plurality in the Electoral College. Shortly after the general election vote on 6 November 1860, Southern states began to secede, the first being South Carolina.

For many of you who have seen the world-renowned movie or read the book, *Gone With The Wind*, do you remember the scene at the Wilkes' Twelve Oaks Plantation during the barbecue, where they had just received word that the Georgia Legislature had voted secession? Georgia officially seceded in January 1861. As war fever gripped the men, they rushed to kiss their sweethearts, jumped onto their horses, and were off to war. The people were so excited and expected to defend their homeland for Southern honor and states' rights. I thought it was the greatest story ever told when I was little. It was the fall of 1971, and eighth grade had just started in late August, when I began to read my most cherished new possession, *Gone With The Wind* by Margaret Mitchell. I was very excited because my mom had joined the Doubleday Book Club. Mom and I had very carefully gone through the brochure choices and she let me get a book. This book by Margaret Mitchell was beautiful, with 719 pages and the smallest print I had ever seen! Little did I know that my love of Civil War history would eventually see me finishing a Masters' Degree in History, working as an Adjunct Professor at our community college, or teaching American History in high school.

It was a cold 38 degrees on this particular Thanksgiving Day in 1971, with no snow on the ground. I have always loved Thanksgiving; as my very talkative family gathered around our bountiful table, it was another chance to hear more wonderful stories about days gone by. Aunt Florence, Uncle Willard, and Grandma Geneva came many times and celebrated this blessed holiday with wonderful food. After dinner, we all retired into the living room around the fireplace and had much great conversation and merriment. It was always about 5 p.m. when our loved ones left; and at this time, I can remember running to my room, flying onto my beautiful canopy bed, and jumping under my fluffy bed covers, only to read the last of what became my most cherished book. Throughout the book, I pictured my ancestors in the story, with my great-great-grandfather Elijah on his plantation, and all his children surrounding him, enjoying a wonderful summer barbecue.

By the time I had finished the book, on 25 November 1972, I had fallen in love with the Civil War Era. My dear mother loved that book, as did all of her four sisters, from whom I had also heard a great deal about the film adaption that had debuted on Friday, 15 December 1939 in Atlanta, Georgia. Since this was back in the day, we didn't have home video, so we had to wait for a theater to show the film. Finally, sometime in 1973, the film came again to Peoria, Illinois. Much to my delight, my mom took me to see the much-anticipated film. I loved going to the movie theater, as it was such a special treat. We got a large popcorn and soda, and my mom always had to have a Hershey's chocolate bar to go with her popcorn. The movie theater was a grand place with beautiful, plush red carpets; beautiful art-deco-styled lighting; a graceful staircase which led to the second floor; and the smell of fresh popped corn wafting in the air. Everyone was filled with anticipation as we walked through the theater entrance doors and walked down the aisle to find the perfect seat. During this time period, they had ushers that wore special outfits and greeted you as you entered the theater and took your ticket stub.

I can still remember the music playing, as the film began and the huge red velvet curtains opened up and transported us into another world on the big screen. I was totally enraptured by the beautifully-produced film and the big screen. Having just finished the book a few months before, the film left a deep impression on fourteen-year-old me—and I was extremely saddened by all the senseless destruction of war, innocent people dying, beautiful houses burned to the ground, and the crooks who took advantage of people's sorrows. War was not all glory, and this was clearly depicted in the film.

The miserable war would go on for four long, bloody years. According to various historians, this war would be considered a "Modern War" because the military forces used some new technology such as reconnaissance balloons and faster pistols. The telegraph had been invented and refined by Samuel F.B. Morse, and in 1860, Congress passed and President Buchanan signed into law the Pacific Telegraph Act, mandating that Secretary of Treasury procure bids for the construction of transcontinental telegraph. This was completed in October 1861, and it merged all telegraph companies into Western Union.[6] The Civil War would see use of armored ships, mine warfare, aerial observations using air balloons, and repeating weapons used by Union soldiers.

According to Burke Davis in *Our Incredible Civil War*, there were many partisan names for the Civil War, from both the North and the South, with their respective biases. The Northerners have called the event the War for the Union, the Great Rebellion, the Southern Rebellion, the War of the Rebellion, and the War of Southern Planters. The Southerners have called the war the Lost Cause, the War for Southern Freedom, the Confederate War, the War for Nationality, the War for Southern Rights, the War for States' Rights, the War for Constitutional Liberty, Mr. Lincoln's War, the Second American War for Independence, the War of Secession, the War for Separation, the Yankee Invasion, the War to Suppress Yankee Aggression, the War against Northern Aggression, the War for Southern

Independence, the War between the States, and the Civil War Between the States.[7]

Living in Virginia, I have always been in wonderment that we are so close to what were the original colonies, with many genealogies linked from pioneer families traveling the great Wagon Road from Pennsylvania to the South. As such, many Virginians had immediate family members in Pennsylvania, Maryland, and Washington, D.C., our nation's capital. The Commonwealth of Virginia did not take the decision to secede lightly, but unfortunately, the economic ways of life were linked with North Carolina and the South. During my graduate degree studies, I can remember studying about how Virginia and North Carolina were so much alike throughout the early colonial era that there was much consternation in forming a boundary between the Carolinas and Virginia. (If you have ever really looked at the southern boundary of Virginia, it is as straight as it could possibly have been, due to the diligence of William Byrd, of Westover Plantation along the James River.)

I believe such deep familial ties with the Middle Atlantic colonies is one of the main reasons that Virginia was one of the last states to secede, on 17 April 1861, followed by Arkansas, North Carolina, and Tennessee. The vote for secession had taken place just days before Elijah enlisted because of the Virginia General Assembly's beliefs about states' rights. A great deal of the war was fought in Virginia, north through Maryland into Pennsylvania. Currently, Congress has designated the area from Gettysburg, Pennsylvania to Charlottesville, Virginia as having the most historic sites, and the Civil War Trust has done a great job promoting tourism and preservation of these sites. As you drive along the route from the Battle of Gettysburg to

Charlottesville, Virginia, there are signs announcing "Hallowed Ground." The project, called "Journey Through the Hallowed Ground", was sponsored by Civil War Trust Organization and honors all soldiers who fought or lost their lives defending their beliefs. The project is looking for biographies of these men who gave their lives to be written and posted on the FOLD3 military site, in conjunction with Ancestry.com. For each biography posted, the project will plant and geo-tag a tree to commemorate service. The project is awesome and needs many biographies written. My students participate in this project because it helps them learn how to read and analyze primary source documents. In preserving our American history, it is our duty to participate when we can.

Virginia would see nearly four long years of bloody fighting on its soil, with approximately 192,924 people, or 12.1 percent of the population, answering that call to duty. It is important to note that due to the nature of recordkeeping during this time period there was no exact science; and as such, different sources vary on numbers. As more archaeological study is conducted, historic findings may differ.[8] In 1860, the population of Virginia was 1,156,318 with 1,047,411 whites, 58,042 free blacks and 490,865 slaves. Virginia had the largest number of free blacks in the country, as well as the largest number of slaves.[9]

CHAPTER 4:
Elijah and His Place in War

As I began retracing this next chapter of Elijah's life, I had no clue where this adventure would take me. Many of the sites are well-within a day's adventure; however, his West Virginia adventures have taken me a little longer to experience, with the greatest distance travelled about 350 miles—almost to Kentucky border, through the very mountainous roads of West Virginia, driving through what seemed to be endless switchbacks.

To the best of my research findings, I have compiled his whereabouts during our American Civil War, based upon his service record in Company K of the 6th Virginia Cavalry and the paths they followed during these few years. I followed his adventures through the towns and villages of Virginia, Maryland, Pennsylvania, and the western part of Virginia, which officially became known as West Virginia in June 1863. It was on the 22 April 1861 that Elijah heard the call of duty to defend his homeland, just like his forefathers before him, and he made his way to Leesburg, Virginia, to enlist in the cavalry, which had been originally organized by Captain Daniel Shreve in June 1858. Coincidentally, this was the same day that Governor John Letcher had appointed Robert E. Lee as the head of all of Virginia's forces, and a few days later, all Confederate forces were placed under the new Commander-in-Chief, Jefferson Davis, who had just been elected as the new Confederate President. Shortly thereafter, President Lincoln included all Virginia and North Carolina ports in the Union blockade of all Confederate Ports. North Carolina did not officially secede until 20 May 1861.[10]

My original plan was to follow Elijah through the chronology of time; however, they rode all over the countryside and towns, back and forth, and this agenda became very difficult to follow. As he was in the cavalry, their horses took them wherever they needed to go. In this part of the adventure, my bright yellow "Willie" jeep with large tires, great tread, four-wheel drive, and ultimately the ability not to get stuck in the mud experienced very narrow dirt roads, steep hills, muddy potholes, deep mud, and open highway. Many of Elijah's routes were definitely off the beaten path, over hill and dale, through many fords of Virginia rivers and mountain gaps—some of which I could not get to, as they are now on private property.

Elijah Enlists in Leesburg (April 1861)

The first part of the journey took me to Leesburg, Virginia, the place where Elijah chose to enlist. The Loudoun Cavalry was part of the 6th Virginia Cavalry Regiment, which subsequently became named Company K, 6th Regiment Virginia Cavalry. The 6th Regiment Cavalry was originally formed of seven independent companies which were assigned by Special Order No. 276A & I.G.O., dated 12 September 1861. Three other companies were subsequently added and the regiment completed its organization in November 1861.[10] Many don't realize this, but there were Union supporters, called "Unionists," who formed regiments in all the Southern states to fight against the Confederacy. There was one Unionist Regiment raised in Loudoun County, Virginia, known as the Loudoun Independent Rangers, composed of 800 white men, mostly from the western part of the county, of German and Quaker ancestry. They acted primarily as guerilla warriors and, in Virginia, they confronted the Confederates at Lovettsville, Middleburg, Upperville, and Waterford, until the Shenandoah Valley Campaign of 1864 when they fought with the Union Army. Each Southern state, except for South Carolina, had at least one Unionist group.[2] As Elijah enlisted and was present on 30 April 1861, one can only imagine what excitement or fear was going through his mind. How many of his childhood friends heard that same call of duty and joined him? Where were his cousins? It wasn't very long before the men were called to action.

As we moved along to see the next part of the journey, we continued up Route 15 North and crossed the Potomac River, which is the official dividing line between Maryland and Virginia. The river begins in the Appalachian Mountains and flows into the Chesapeake Bay about 380 miles later. On 5 July 1861, five men from Elijah's Company K forded the Potomac River (as there was no beautiful paved bridge to cross) at Heater's Island and captured some Federal Troops from the 1st New Hampshire

Heators Island, Potomac River. Photo by G. Lindner

Infantry Union. Pickets were placed here on this small island in the middle of the Potomac.[10] Heater's Island was originally a Native American camp, which John Smith had visited on his explorations to Virginia on the Potomac River in 1608.

As the summer of 1861 continued, it was high society season. Mrs. Lincoln held wonderful, very lavish events at the White House in Washington, D.C., and President Lincoln professed his earnest belief that Union troops, also known as Federal troops, would gain control of the Confederates in ninety days and normalcy would return. With the dawn 12 April 1861 brought the beginning of the thirty-four-hour skirmish at Fort Sumter in South Carolina, where the Confederates had taken the U.S. Military fort and would not surrender. Mr. Lincoln called up the troops for ninety days to take back the fort because he believed any insurrections could be easily put down. Many folks believed this, as Washington, D.C. was a hotbed of gossip and everyone wanted to be entertained and watch the Yankees beat the Rebels—nothing short of a great baseball game.

In these early days, many people did not understand the magnitude of what was happening and totally underestimated the Confederates on their reasons for secession. With that being said, in July 1861 the nation would see the first real battle of the war in Manassas, Virginia, also known as the First Battle of Bull Run. This was the biggest news in months, and people came out to cheer their team on for the surprise Yankee attack. The spectators included Congressmen with their families, many couples, and other people who did not want to miss the first fireworks. They took a leisurely carriage or wagon drive out from the city, about a three-hour drive by carriage, with picnics in tow. Not surprisingly, the city was a hotbed of

House which served as a Hospital at the First Battle of Bull Run, aka The First Battle of Manassas. Photo by G. Lindner

spies, but no one figured the rebels would know about this surprise attack. As the beautiful ladies began spreading out their quilts for their memorable picnic up on the hillside, bullets and cannonballs soon began flying, rather close to where they chose to watch the battle from. Needless to say, both civilians and soldiers retreated as fast as they could to Washington, D.C. Horses were going haywire as the cannonballs were exploding right before their very eyes.

In July and August 1861, Elijah was present for Muster Roll, having been paid through July 1861 by Captain Shreve. General Thomas "Stonewall" Jackson arrived with his Brigade on 19 July, ready for battle on 21 July and the aftermath 22 and 23 July. General Jackson would earn his nickname "Stonewall" at this battle, as he stood firm in the face of battle, encouraging his men to do their best; not once did he waiver.

On 21 July 1861, Elijah and the Loudoun Cavalry were present to do their part in protecting their homeland at the First Battle of Manassas, and they helped pursue the Yankees down Route 29 East to Washington, D.C. I have visited this battle site many times throughout the last twenty-five years, and I have always felt a draw to the site, but never knew why until I learned that my Elijah was part of this battle.[10]

After the First Battle of Manassas, their journey took them to Point of Rocks, where the bridge crossed the Potomac River into Maryland. Earlier in the summer, they had ridden the same path; however, this time they used White's Ferry to cross the Potomac to save some time. On 5 August 1861, the company was stationed around Point of Rocks; they were attacked by sixty Yankees, left with one dead with six wounded. George Orrison was the first soldier killed in Loudoun County. New units were constantly forming, and on 12 September 1861, the Loudoun Company was officially formed by Special Order #276, Paragraph 16 of The Adjutant and Inspector Generals Office, Headquarters, Virginia Forces, 12 September 1861.[10]

The Battle of Ball's Bluff (October 1861)

The Battle of Ball's Bluff took place just outside of Leesburg, Virginia on 21 October 1861. As I drove into the site, I noticed that it has been beautifully preserved with many tall trees; the hilly landscape is absolutely beautiful. There is a small cemetery that commemorates those who gave their lives in service of their respective side. I believe this is the smallest of our national cemeteries. Ball's Bluff sits high upon a ridge overlooking the Potomac River. It is a beautiful, peaceful site, and it has been very well preserved. In this altercation, Elijah and his 6th Virginia Cavalry did not see any direct battle action; however, they were in reserve waiting to be called upon as reinforcements were needed, situated near Edward's Ferry.[11]

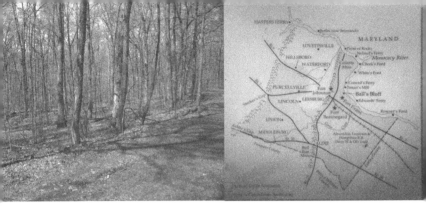

Balls Bluff. Photo by G. Lindner

The Federal troops had to cross the Potomac River here in order to pass into Virginia. Keep in mind that even though Maryland had slaves, they did not secede with the rest of the Southern States. Union General McClellan had sent Union General Charles Stone to scout out Confederates who were under the command of Confederate Colonel Nathan Evans near Leesburg, Virginia. The Union soldiers were placed under unrealistic expectations of a very novice commanding officer, Captain Chase Philbrick.[11] Unlike Philbrick, Colonel Evans was an experienced battle commander. The Federal troops tried climbing up the very steep bluff overlooking the Potomac River, but were driven back. Apparently, on a reconnaissance mission in the night before, Philbrick had believed he saw a small Confederate Camp. When he took a small number of troops back over the river the next morning, what he thought were tents were in fact just trees. While they were there, they ran into a Confederate patrol, which ignited the battle. As a result, many Federal Soldiers drowned and even more surrendered, rather than being thrown in the river.[11]

The war progressed at a rapid rate, and at this early stage, the Confederates were winning, due to incompetent Union

Generals and the fact that they were fighting for their homeland. The next encounter would be only miles from where Elijah had grown up, and they seemed to be placed in the thick of the battle action. By November 1861, the entire Virginia Cavalry regiment was officially complete and all companies had received their Alpha designator. The Commanding Officer selected was Charles William Field. It had been only months since Elijah took an oath, and in that short time, they had seen a lot of action. In early December 1861, the 6th Virginia Cavalry regiment departed Leesburg and marched to Centreville, arriving on 5 December for their winter camp.[10]

Today, there are still many historical landmarks that can be seen at the camp. When I found the remaining corner- stone of Fort Johnson there, and some trenches, it all seemed

Centreville Encampment at Mount Gilead Inn.
Photo by G. Lindner

so peaceful. The trenches have been preserved in this small, off- the-beaten-path wooded area, near the well-preserved historic Mount Gilead Inn, which dates back as far as 1760. This very peaceful area saw some horrific happenings during the war. It was here that Elijah and his Cavalry joined Field's Regiment and officially became Company K, part of Confederate General J. E. B. Stuart's Brigade. Elijah was paid by the Regiment's Quarter- master, Captain Carter, until 1 December 1861.

At this point in time, he decided to reenlist and he received a furlough for thirty days from 11 February 1862. Because of this furlough, Elijah was absent from the first muster of the New Year, taken in 1862 for January through February. During his well-deserved furlough, Company K was searching Leesburg, Virginia for deserters.[10]

As Elijah and his cavalry waited out the winter—completing drills, mending clothes, playing soldier games, and taking care of their horses—they were on constant lookout because the Yankees were never far away. Soldiers were confined to Camp Smith during this time, located in Centreville, Virginia at the intersection of Route 29 West and Route 28 North. During their time in winter quarters, the soldiers passed the time by playing various games and training. Unfortunately, disease was rampant and some took ill and died. Commanding officers also sent riders to locate missing soldiers and deserters, and posted a reward of $30 per deserter. These times were difficult for the men; their morale was low, and they saw friends die of diseases like typhoid fever. I imagine Company K was very happy to depart camp on 11 January 1862 for Leesburg, Virginia, in an effort to find missing soldiers from other regiments.[10] Centreville saw a lot of action during the first few years of the war, and this small crossroads town changed hands six times during the war. In March 1862, Confederate General Joseph Johnston moved his troops to Fredericksburg, while Confederate General Richard S. Ewell was sent to march West, then South, ultimately marching to the peninsula in Virginia to protect Richmond.[10] This Virginia Peninsula was located between the York and the James Rivers, and was one of the major approaches into the Confederate Capital of Richmond, which had been moved from Montgomery, Alabama to Richmond, Virginia.

Shenandoah Campaign (April 1862)

In late April 1862, Company K and the Brigade traveled through Swift Run Gap in Virginia along their route to the Shenandoah Valley, where they were assigned to serve under General Stonewall Jackson as reinforcements for the Valley Campaign. They met up with him after they crossed Massanutten Mountain at Luray, Virginia.[10] Swift Run Gap, a wind gap, is one of four thoroughfares across the Blue Ridge Mountains, which are part of Appalachian Mountain chain. The Gap crosses Skyline Drive, which is a well-loved 109 mile seasonal fall drive along the ridge of the Blue Ridge Mountains, built in the 1930's by the Civilian Conservation Corps, as part of Franklin D. Roosevelt's New Deal Program.

As we ventured out to experience Swift Run Gap, I was a bit apprehensive, as I get nervous driving through the mountains. However, I really enjoyed driving along Route 33 West. Route 33 was originally known as the Spotswood Trail, named for Alexander Spotswood, who served as Virginia's Lieutenant Governor in 1710, and later as the Governor. During his tenure, he sent out a group of soldiers and sailors to capture and kill the notorious Blackbeard the Pirate; the group was successful. The Virginia Assembly named Spotsylvania County and a major E-W thoroughfare road after him. I was pleasantly surprised to find this historical mountain road had very spacious roads on the switchbacks through the mountain. On this particular day while driving, much to our dislike, we saw in the Southern distance smoke rising out of the Shenandoah Mountains, and later heard a major forest fire had started during the time we passed through the gap. This fire was one of the park's worst fires in eighty years, and destroyed more than 8,000 parkland acres. Another aside is that Skyline Drive was built as one of Franklin Roosevelt's New Deal initiatives during the 1930's, runs about 105 miles through the Blue Ridge Mountains, and is most beautiful in the spring and the fall.

As we continued our enjoyable drive, we passed onto another Elijah route and found beautiful mountain scenery, all from the comfort of the open-top Jeep, with the wind blowing and the sun brightly shining. However, I can only imagine how Elijah felt after that long ride on his beloved sorrel mare, which he brought from home when he enlisted. Under the command of Confederate Colonel Thomas T. Munford, Company K was positioned at the end of the Brigade for the march west, then south. We decided to follow it and continued towards Massanutten Mountain.

As we approached Massanutten Mountain, we were in awe of the beauty of the age-old geographical landmark. Today, there is a huge, very popular resort that each year sees thousands of visitors, though I can say with confidence that Elijah was not thinking "ski resort" when he was passing through. First off, although skiing had been popular in other parts of the world, during Elijah's life and as early as 1850, skis were used primarily to deliver mail from Idaho to Northern California. It must have been a true pleasure to ride a horse in the snows; however, in May 1862, the worst that he and the entire 6th Cavalry rode through was rain and mud in this area as they crossed the pass across the Blue Ridge Mountains to join forces with General Stonewall Jackson in Luray, Virginia. Elijah and his company K served as a screening detachment, looking for an unusual action. These encounters were all part of the 1862 Shenandoah Valley Campaign.

On the evening of 30 April 1862 in New Market, Virginia, the 6th Cavalry along with their brigade joined General Jackson's Corps. Union General George McClellan and his Army of the Potomac had marched his troops to prepare for battle in the Peninsular Campaign. McClellan's goal was to move his troops between the Confederate troops and take over Richmond, the Confederate capital.[10]

In New Market, the Confederates used a variety of strategies to make the Union Army believe the Rebels had more soldiers than they actually did. The 6th Virginia Cavalry and the 2nd Virginia Cavalry both made a stand here and convinced Union General Nathaniel Banks that General Jackson's Corps were all present, when in fact General Jackson had taken the rest of the Corps and marched west via Parkersburg Road to defeat Union General John C. Frémont at the Battle of McDowell at the bottom of the Bull Pasture Mountain. As with most mountains, there is a river named for the Bull Pasture Mountain. Apparently, Bullpasture River is an excellent place for fishing, and eventually flows into the famous James River, named for King James II and Jamestown.[12]

At the Battle of McDowell, the Confederates were positioned on Sitlington's Hill, near the top of the mountain, located in Highland County, West Virginia. The battle went on for hours, resulting in a Confederate victory, but not without sacrifice. The Confederates lost nearly twice as many casualties as the Union. Today, the site has been well-preserved, and you can take a two-hour hike along Sitlington's Hill; yes, it is another steep hill. Upon the conclusion of the Battle of McDowell, General Jackson marched against the Union forces that were threatening the Shenandoah Valley in Virginia, along the Great Wagon Road.

McDowell, VA—Sitlington's Hill. Confederate site of Fort Johnson. Photo by G. Lindner

This great valley was called the Breadbasket of the Confederacy because of its rich, wholesome soil, where hearty grains were grown for the Army's fresh bread and a host of other items.[12]

After we left this battle site, little did I expect the extensive high hills and deep valleys that we were about to really experience in the landscape of Highland County, Virginia. This geographical landform possesses many mountains and valleys, which is why this county is often referred to as Virginia's Switzerland. Personally, this drive was worse than the one I experienced in driving through the Alps in Switzerland. I have no idea how school buses can travel over those roads in snow and rain; nor where people go for entertainment, food, or a mall. That being said, they live a peaceful life. I saw more "No Trespassing" signs and barbed wire than anywhere I have traveled.

As we were driving in these mountains the one thing that really surprised me was the size of the bugs—big yellow bugs—with their loud splat on my windshield. Throughout our journey through the mountains, the bugs were very attracted to the yellow Jeep. As we drove on and on throughout the mountains that I never thought were going to end, the most exciting find of the drive was on the top of Shenandoah Mountain, where Highland County and Augusta County meet. Off to the

The Shenandoah Mountain Lookout   *Confederate Breastworks. Photo by G. Lindner*

left of the road, we saw a lookout vantage point and a historical sign (yes, we tried to stop at every historical sign we see because we don't want to miss any historical event!).

We pulled up in the parking lot and were lucky that the afternoon was just beautiful, with a sparkling blue sky and very pleasant climate. Lo and behold, we had serendipitously found the Confederate Breastworks Interpretive Trail. Elijah had been here almost exactly 154 years before to the day. I said to my husband, "Wow, this is fantastic! Best find ever!" This site had been very nicely maintained and there was a small outdoor bathroom. I was especially excited because we hadn't seen any bathrooms for quite a while and it is difficult to just pull off the road like they did back in the day. I quickly got out of the Jeep, ran over to the small facility, and opened the door. What I saw was unbelievable. Every bee and fly within miles that had not become a victim on my windshield was buzzing around that bathroom. No way was I going to let this special moment be spoiled by a few bugs! I felt as though I had really connected with Elijah through the distance of time, so I decided to rough it just like Elijah did. Problem solved. As I walked around, I could not believe the beauty of the moment. I stood there, looking at the same peaceful mountains that so many before had experienced. The view was unbelievable; the Confederates could have seen for miles and miles. The breastworks and Fort Edward Johnson, named after Confederate Brigadier General Edward Johnson, were built by about 3,000 troops in the spring of 1862. By the end of May, Elijah had arrived with General Jackson. The breastworks were constructed by the Confederates to defend their beloved breadbasket against a federal invasion. Today, the Fort is nothing more than a sign and some marked rocks, but nevertheless, the view from the sign that was once Fort Johnson was absolutely breathtaking.

While driving through the Breadbasket, down I-81 South, we marveled at the beauty of the mountains we had just driven across from Elkton, West Virginia, and of the foothills, which were very open and refreshing. In order to continue along the path of the 6th Virginia Cavalry, we departed the Interstate just outside of Harrisonburg, Virginia (where James Madison University is) to go east along Route 33. I shared with you earlier our delightful drive along Virginia's Route 33, which has certainly become one of my favorite roads to take a drive along to the I-81 corridor.

While we traveled again on this road, I kept remembering how in 1862, Elijah had traveled many times on this very same road. Our destination was Newton, Virginia, where his 6th Virginia Cavalry, along with the 2nd Virginia Cavalry, went to complete another mission. If you're following along with us on a map, be advised that after the war in 1867, the Postal Service of Newton, Virginia changed the name from Newton to Stephens City, Virginia. In Newton, they assisted with the capture of many wagons and horses, and about 225 men. This little town was founded in 1732 by German immigrants along the Philadelphia Great Wagon Road, just south of the town of Winchester, Virginia in the Lower Shenandoah Valley. It was originally nicknamed New-Town, while also known as Stephensburg. Eyewitnesses report that on 24 May 1862, the town changed hands six times on between the Union and Confederate forces. The Union Army burned houses and wrought havoc and fear on the residents.[13] At this point in the Shenandoah Campaign, General Jackson was forced to retreat because the Federals were closing in on his Corps on three sides. On 29 May 1862, faced with very few options, he marched his forces and advanced to Charles Town in Jefferson County, Virginia, which was strategically located at the entrance to the Shenandoah. Jackson moved with the Brigade and the twelve prisoners captured by the 6th Virginia Cavalry, which was again among the troops who were in the rear of the Corps.[10]

Battles of Port Republic and Cross Keys (June 1862)

Elijah traveled through Strasburg, Virginia on 1 June 1862 during the evening hours when Union General Frémont launched an attack on the Rebels near Strasburg, Virginia. Sadly, Colonel George H. Stuart, the senior officer in command of the Confederate 2nd Virginia Cavalry and the 6th Virginia Cavalry, badly bungled the retreat and caused a stampede of soldiers. As a result, the regiment was transferred from General J. E. B. Stuart's command to General Turner Ashby.[10]

Our trip to Strasburg was very interesting and I was very excited to see the old train station there. I had hoped there would be an actual Civil War Era train. When we arrived, it had just finished snowing, so the tiny, very hilly mountain roads were beautiful. When we arrived at the train station, we discovered that the train was just a wooden replica. I was so disappointed. We got our photos and continued following Elijah's path of retreat.

Later in the week after the retreat from Strasburg, on 6 June 1862, Elijah's group was ambushed by Federals while riding along Port Republic Road, just outside of Harrisonburg, Virginia. They were chased for over a mile, across a boggy creek, when they soon realized the serious need for the infantry to take the ambushing group. As they charged, they found themselves smack dab in front of the Union Line.[10] What a surprise this must have been!

The Confederate Stonewall Brigade rejoined General Jackson's Brigade at a bridge across the South Fork of the Shenandoah River at Port Republic in Rockingham County. The Shenandoah River, a tributary of the mighty Potomac River, is a beautiful, sparkly, clean river, which consists of the North Fork and the South Fork, each being about 100 miles long. The next day, Brigadier General Samuel Winder's brigade attacked Union forces on the eastern part of the river in what is known as the Battle of Port Republic.[14] After several counterattacks by both sides, Winder captured five pieces of artillery and turned them against the rest of the Union line. Union Major General Erasmus B. Tyler ordered a withdrawal about 10:30 a.m. [10]

Because he expected Union General Frémont to cross the river and attack him on the following day, Confederate General "Stonewall" Jackson chose to withdraw through the woods and consolidate his army near Mount Vernon Furnace.

However, during the night, Union General Frémont moved instead to Harrisonburg. The Battle at Port Republic cost the most lives of any battle fought by General Jackson's Army of the Valley during its Shenandoah Campaign.[15]

The old saying that "there is no rest for the weary" definitely held true for the 6th Virginia. The next day, 8 June, Elijah and the rest of the 6th Virginia were protecting the train carrying the Confederate Baggage. Along the way, they tailed the enemy while collecting food, munitions, and badly needed wagons. The 6th Virginia spent two days completing this task in what is known as the Battle of Cross Keys.[10] Port Republic and the Battle of Cross Keys saw the Confederate Army of the Valley winning the Upper and Middle Shenandoah Valley.[14] Further, General Jackson was able to march to assist Confederate General Robert E. Lee and his Army of Northern Virginia before they marched southeast to Richmond.[16]

The 6th Virginia Cavalry was to meet Jackson in Richmond, and they took the break in action to muster on 30 June 1862. Elijah was present on this day and was paid for his time between 28 February 1862 and 30 June 1862. His previous paycheck had been paid for the period between 30 April 1861 and 31 December 1861. Also during this month, the leadership of the 6th Virginia Cavalry changed; General Beverly H. Robinson replaced Colonel Munford, the commanding officer of the 6th Virginia Cavalry, as he had been promoted to General for political reasons.[17]

As they traveled southeast to meet General Jackson in Richmond, just imagine the summer heat and humidity they experienced with their wool uniforms and the heavy gear they were carrying, which averaged a weight of fifty pounds. As I traveled this route in the present day, I was very comfortable, with plenty of water and snacks, commenting on the beautiful scenery and rolling hills around us. Even today, driving this route, we felt like we were in the middle of nowhere.

In July 1862, the 6th Virginia Cavalry and the entire Brigade joined up with General Jackson's Corps, just outside of the Confederate Capital of Richmond, Virginia. On 10 July, the Brigade marched west to Gordonsville to confront Union forces under the command of General John Pope. On 16 July, Colonel Thomas Stanhope Flournoy joined Elijah in the 6th Virginia Cavalry. The end of the month, 27 July, saw the 6th Virginia serving picket duty on the upper fords of the Rapidan River.[10] If you ever get the opportunity to tour this beautiful area of Culpeper County in Virginia, you will find some of the best Virginia wineries and a couple of distilleries which contribute to Virginia tourism.

Rivers and geographic landforms played an important part of the Civil War. In the Eastern Theatre of the Civil War, the Rapidan River played a critical role; and in its entirety, meanders over eighty miles through farmlands across the Virginia countryside. As you may wonder how the river received its name, according to early settlers, the river flowed rapidly. Queen Anne of Great Britain and Ireland, niece of King Charles II, served as the sovereign from May 1707 until August 1714. The Rapidan River eventually flows into the Rappahannock River to the west of Fredericksburg, Virginia. The Rappahannock River begins its journey in Thomas Jefferson's beloved Blue Ridge Mountains, and flows east for about 180 miles from the mountains into Chesapeake Bay, located south of the Potomac River. Early Virginia saw many settlements along this flowing river. During the

Civil war, the river served as the site for many war campaigns; in 1862, both the Battle at Rappahannock Station and the Battle of Fredericksburg took place along this river. This river offered some fords that both armies used, and I was able to get to a few of these fords, but the most important ford, Morton's Ford, is on private property, so I was not able to see it.

Around this time, on 17 July 1862, President Lincoln signed into law the Militia Draft Act. He announced the draft on 4 August 1862. Consequently, the Conscription Act, passed by Congress, was signed into law 16 February 1863.[9] There was much debate in Congress on exemptions, alien eligibility, draft avoidance, and riots. According to E.B. Long in *The Civil War Day by Day*, men in the North were self-mutilating or escaping to Canada to avoid being drafted. In the South, Confederate President Jefferson Davis approved the Conscription Bill on 16 April 1862, which had been passed by the Confederate Congress.[9]

Second Battle of Manassas Campaign (1862)

At this point, the war action became very exciting and quite intense for the next few weeks. As I sat in front of Madison Courthouse, one beautiful, sunny pleasant Virginia day, I closed my eyes, travelling back in time to that very busy day at this site on 8 August 1862.[10] A group of Confederate cavalry would have passed by in pursuit of the Union cavalry five miles down the winding country road. They were thwarting a regrouping of the Union cavalry, which had occupied Madison Courthouse with the purpose of guarding several fords of the Rapidan River.

These Federal units were attempting to advance towards General Stonewall Jackson's left flank as they marched northward, taking only one Confederate soldier as Prisoner by the Federals.[10]

The next day, 9 August 1862, Elijah and the 6th Virginia arrived at the Battle of Cedar Mountain and stood ready to participate, but were ultimately not needed. Union General Nathaniel Banks had attacked General Stonewall Jackson's corps that was waiting north of the Rapidan River and south of the town of Culpepper.[10] Interestingly, Cedar Mountain was nick-named Slaughter Mountain by the Confederates. The next day, 10 August, the 6th Virginia spent their day looking for Union troops in the area of Culpeper

Out of all of my adventures in finding Elijah, I really enjoyed the charm that Culpeper offered. As a matter of fact, I was shocked! I couldn't believe I had never been to this lovely small town, only forty miles away from my home. In looking for Elijah's footsteps, my goal was to drive to Culpeper Court House, take a photo, and move on with the journey. As we

Cedar Mountain, VA. Photo by G. Lindner

entered town, we decided to follow the signs to the tourist information center, which just happened to be the old train station, still in use. The current station was built in 1904, which replaced two prior buildings on that site, both burned down, with the very first station built in 1854. I went to the front desk, and the two ladies in charge were extremely friendly and helpful. I am very appreciative that Mrs. Karen Quaintance, the Visitor Center Assistant, spent a lot of time with me, answering questions about the town and Cedar Mountain Battlefield. Her help was invaluable; she directed me to a very detailed hand-drawn map of Culpeper, where Elijah and his 6th Virginia Cavalry saw a great deal of excitement. The hand-drawn map was unbelievable, and when I asked her if I could take photos of it, she told me I could go just down the street to the library and purchase one.

I really wanted to take a photo of the Culpeper Court House, as Elijah was there; however, she told me the building had actually been moved! How can you move a courthouse? Sadly, that is the price small towns pay for modernization.

For many years, the passenger train stopped at the station for a couple of hours while the passengers got off the train, walked across the tracks, and had lunch at an old hotel, which no longer stands. She had so much knowledge to share about the town, and showed me a book on Culpeper County, which the visitor center just happened to sell for $10. Sold! By the time we finished our conversation, I was very excited to explore the tiny streets and old buildings and find a special place to dine. We found the cutest little cheese store to eat lunch, Culpeper Cheese Company. As we entered this adorable store, we were immediately drawn to a counter where they were giving out samples of cheeses made in Virginia. As a cheese lover, I really enjoyed this experience, so we decided to have lunch. The menu had some very interesting, eclectic panini sandwiches. I highly recommend the Sumptuous Spain Panini, a carefully constructed with grilled delight with Manchego cheese, chorizo, roasted pepper, topped off with a very tasty olive tapenade. The menu also offered gluten-free and vegetarian paninis. There were some very interesting items in the store you could purchase, from local Virginia wines to out-of-the-ordinary crackers. We are definitely going back to try everything on their menu. At this point, I would like to tell you that though we ordered a great bottle of wine, it wasn't a "wine" kind of outing, because we were touring.

Elijah's adventure to Culpeper was not quite as leisurely as mine. Sometime around 17 August 1862, the 6th Virginia reached the town, and upon their arrival, the Culpeper Ladies greeted the 6th Virginia with a tub full of homemade lemonade. It was commonly rumored and well-known that General Stonewall Jackson loved lemons, as he reportedly sucked on a lemon just before a battle. A good time was certainly had by all, and apparently the ladies told sordid true tales of "vile and licentious behaviors" put forth by a group of Union General Pope's soldiers.[9]

As you know, southern men prided themselves on defending the honor of a lady, so after a much-enjoyed respite from battle, the Brigade attacked the enemy cavalry between

Culpeper, VA. The Train Station. Photo by G. Lindner

Stevensburg and Brandy Station, and the Federals were forced to retreat back to Fleetwood Hill. At that time, Elijah saw yet another change to his commanding officers in the 6th Virginia Cavalry. General J. E. B. Stuart was given command of all Confederate Cavalry in General Robert E. Lee's Army of Northern Virginia. A few days later, on 20 August, 6th Virginia crossed the Rapidan River again to look for and observe Union General Pope's forces. The 6th Virginia held one of the flanks and they forced the Federals back across the river. After the battle, the 6th Virginia Cavalry returned to Culpeper and met up with the Simms Family. A member of the Cavalry is reputed to have shouted, "Ladies, your wrongs have been avenged."[10]

The group had no time to rest on their laurels, but continued their pursuit of the enemy. On 22 August 1862, the cavalry forded the Rappahannock River, entered Warrenton, and then rode to Catlett Station, which is a stop on the Orange and Alexandria Railroad. There were skirmishes between the Union's Army of the Potomac under the Command of General John Pope and the Confederate Army of Northern Virginia under the command of General Robert E. Lee. At Catlett, Elijah and the 6th Virginia assisted in the capture of

Catlett Station, VA— Popes' Headquarters. Photo by G. Lindner

General Pope's headquarters, along with documents, baggage, and 300 prisoners of war. The rain was very heavy, and it was night, so they decided not to destroy the railroad bridge. These actions prompted General Pope to retreat his forces to the Rappahannock River.[10]

By 23 August 1862, Confederate General J. E. B. Stuart completed his raids on Catlett Station. Due to heavy rain and darkness, he returned to the Confederate line on the southern side of the Rappahannock River with the 6th, 7th and 12th Virginia Cavalries, via Fauquier County by White Sulphur Springs, near Warrenton.[10] Because of the heavy rains, it was difficult to ford the river at any random point, and it was even more difficult for the Confederate forces because General Pope's forces controlled all the fords that crossed the Rappahannock River. When they reached Sulphur Springs, the Union pickets had burned the bridge, and then attacked the Confederate forces. Many men were mortally wounded here, in what was called the First Battle of Rappahannock Station (a.k.a., Waterloo Bridge, White Sulphur Springs, Lee Springs, or Freeman's Ford).[9] Sadly, Confederate Lt. Charles William Thrift was actually hit by a cannonball, which cut off his left arm and almost cut his entire body in half. Skirmishes would continue for a couple of days.[10]

When the fighting finally subsided, the boys were able to rest up a few days in their campsite. However, on 26 August, the next major encounter would be just a mile from where the first major battle of the Civil War had been so bravely fought.[10] This Second Battle of Manassas (or Bull Run) would begin what military historians term the Maryland Campaign, where some of the bloodiest fighting of the war would occur.

On the first day of battle, the 6th Virginia encountered a small Federal force coming up on General Jackson's rear and they successfully ran them off. General James Longstreet arrived with his corps, who had been in the Shenandoah Valley as they marched through Thoroughfare Gap. He positioned his corps on General Jackson's right, while General J. E. B. Stuart's cavalry positioned themselves to the right of General Longstreet's corps. The soldiers of General Jerome Robertson's Brigade—including the 6th Virginia Company K—positioned themselves on the end, far right.

General Stuart's Division marched through Amissville, Virginia to Henson's Mill, where they could ford the Rappahannock River. They rode by way of Salem, Virginia (renamed Marshall), crossed the Bull Run Mountains to Haymarket, and met up with General Jackson's Infantry. Their task was to protect the flanks of the corps as they went forth to take four railroad trains located at Bristow Station, Virginia.[10] The Federals got word that Confederate General Jackson was on his way to capture the three trains; however, one train escaped to Manassas Junction. At Manassas, Confederate forces captured a couple hundred prisoners and commandeered many supplies. It had been a great day for the Confederate Forces, but definitely not a good day for the Union's Army of the Potomac.[10]

The Confederates stood atop Signal Hill in Manassas and used very large flags to communicate with lookouts near Manassas, atop both Henry Hill and the Van Pelt Home site. On a clear day, it is beautiful—you can see miles and miles of countryside, including the Blue Ridge Mountains. Just a mile or so down the road, on 29 August, Elijah and his 6th Virginia Cavalry were positioned for the Battle at Groveton. Before the

2nd Bull of Run at Groveton, VA. Photo by G. Lindner

battle, Company K was in the front, leading the way to Haymarket. At Haymarket, they realized that General Jackson was facing General John Pope's Army, the Army of Virginia (this campaign was the only campaign where the Army of Virginia existed). They turned back and General Stuart's entire cavalry was positioned to protect the right flank of the corps.[10]

Darkness had fallen and they were in position for battle. As Confederate General Longstreet's men began arriving the morning of 29 August, Jackson placed 20,000 men, including Company K, south of Stony Ridge on the right flank. Several Federal assaults failed to dislodge the Confederate forces. More miscommunication ensued between Pope and his corps commanders, so that he had no idea that Longstreet was arriving or that his attacks were failing. Jackson attacked north of the turnpike at 6 p.m., just when Pope ordered withdrawal of his troops in that area to cross the highway to defend the Henry House Hill artillery and infantry units. At 8 p.m., he ordered a retreat on the turnpike to Centreville. The tired Confederates, low on ammunition, did not pursue in the darkness.[10]

After the days of heavy fighting, at nightfall of 30 August 1862, the major action of the Second Battle of Manassas finally ended. About 3 p.m. the following day, General Robertson's Brigade, along with four large artillery batteries, advanced forward, inflicting numerous casualties on the Union. Confederate General Stuart's Division was engaged with Union General Popes retreating Army.[10]

Although Lee won the battle, he had not destroyed Pope's army. All in all, among the 48,500 Confederates fighting, they had 9,197 casualties: 1,481 killed, 7,627 wounded, and 89 missing, according to E.B. Long. On the other side, out of the 75,500 Union soldiers, there were 16,054 casualties: 1,724 killed, 8,372 wounded, and 5,958 missing in action.[9]

The Battle of Antietam and the Emancipation Proclamation (September 1862)

As you can only imagine, Union supporters were wondering how the Army of Virginia under the Command of General John Pope, a small part of the entire Army of the Potomac commanded by General McClellan, could perform so badly, being so close to the capital. What was that General doing?

President Abraham Lincoln was beside himself, especially after he heard a rumor that the British had sent numerous troops to Canada and were beginning preparedness operations in Halifax at The Citadel to help the South win the war. Why?

At this point in time, the South was providing ninety percent of the world's cotton and the British were excellent consumers of the cotton. Britain was transporting their troops to mainland Canada; from there they could enter the war. The threat of the Confederate Army of Northern Virginia taking over Washington D.C., the U.S. capital city, became more real every day. President Lincoln needed to have a plan in place to prevent the British from assisting the Cotton Kingdom of the South with resources and manpower.

The Maryland Campaign was now in full swing. After the Second Battle of Manassas, on 7 September, Company K rode west to Warrenton and then onto Salem (Marshall) looking for lost Confederates. As a result of this mission, they did not continue the northward movement with the rest of the Confederacy to the Battle of Antietam in Sharpsburg, Maryland at this time.[10] That was the bloodiest single-day battle in American history, with over 22,000 casualties, and the first battle on Union soil.[9] Though General Lee's army was outnumbered two to one, he kept fighting until a standstill, at which point on 19 September, he retreated to Martinsburg, Virginia.[10] Though only a technical victory for the Union because Lee retreated (but no clear winner otherwise), Lincoln used this opportunity to announce his Emancipation Proclamation to discourage foreign governments from recognizing the Confederacy. He also used this victory as a reason to change his chief war aim from preserving the Union to ending slavery.

While all of that as going on, Elijah and the 6th Cavalry had set up a roadblock to guard both Snickers Gap and Ashby's Gap, so the enemy would think there were more troops than there actually were.[10] The Southern troops seemed to be masterful at this ploy and used this strategy often to successfully fool the Union commanders. Snickers Gap, originally William's Gap, is located in the Blue Ridge Mountains, part of the Appalachian Mountain Range, and is a wind gap, bordering Loudoun County and Clarke Counties in Virginia. Ashby's Gap is also a wind gap in the same mountains and borders Fauquier County, Loudoun County, and Clarke County. Throughout the Civil War, both Union and Confederate forces used these gaps during the Shenandoah Campaigns.[9] Near Paris, Virginia, on 22 September 1862, there was an accidental meeting of the 6th Virginia Cavalry with Union Troops. After this very brief skirmish at Ashby's Gap, the 6th Cavalry fled back towards Winchester; however, four men were killed, thirteen wounded and fourteen taken prisoner.[10]

Elijah is Captured (October 1862)

Hold on to your hats, because for the next couple of weeks, Elijah really earned his pay. On Sunday, 28 September, 6th Virginia Cavalry were sent to scout ahead in Loudoun County for Federal Troops passing via Leesburg, Middleburg, and Upperville, reaching Berryville, which is located in the northern part of Shenandoah Valley in Virginia. It began when twenty-one members of the 6th Virginia, Company K, including Elijah, rode about twenty-five miles to Aldie on 9 October, under a very junior officer, Lt. George F. Means. They encountered a Federal Patrol there, which consisted of members from the Unionist 3rd Virginia Cavalry under the command of Lt. S.B. Conger. Instantly, seven poorly-armed men charged and prepared for battle, but Means ordered the

Mountville Intersection, near where Elijah was captured as a prisoner of war.
Photo by G. Lindner

remaining cavalry to halt. There, Lt. Means met his untimely demise, while Private Russell and Sgt. William Ball, Jr. were wounded. The rest retreated seven miles east of Aldie.[10]

It must have been very chaotic, and on 16 October 1862, Elijah was captured by enemy forces of Union Major General Franz Siegel after his horse, a sorrel mare, was shot from under him in Mountville, Virginia, only about twenty-five miles from his home. I can't even imagine the sadness in his heart as he realized his horse, his best friend in the world, who he tenderly cared for daily, was gone. I will never know how long he had owned this horse, as he brought her from home. Elijah wrote to the Confederate Government requesting compensation of his loss of property, which he was granted.

At this point, it is documented that Elijah was captured

in battle; however, in his service record, there is a difference in two dates. This date came from the January/February 1863 Muster Roll: "Captured at the Mountsville, Loudoun Co, VA 9 October 1862 within the enemy's lines." It is interesting to note that these enemy lines were just a few miles from his home. As you will remember, earlier in our story, Elijah had worked in the Aldie Mill, just down the road from his capture. On the Muster Roll Note of 18 October 1862, it says Elijah was captured at Mountville, Loudoun County, Virginia on 16 October 1862.

Was Elijah captured twice, and escaped the first time? Given that he was in very familiar territory, this was possible. Mountville, a community that is spread out and still unincorporated today in Loudoun County, Virginia, is situated on the main branches of Goose Creek and Beaverdam Creek. Mountville is located on the Snickersville Turnpike about halfway between Aldie and Philomont. Snickersville Turnpike was one of two roads that went through the Shenandoah Mountains. The Iroquois Indians used this as their Shenandoah Hunting Path. As we went looking for this place, the roads were very narrow, and the road was sunken. We did cross over some streams, but this place is just a tiny spot where two crossroads come together. There is not a town in sight, but rather a lot of farmland.[10]

As a prisoner, Elijah was transported by wagon from Aldie to the Provost Marshall's office at Fairfax Courthouse, on 19 October 1862, where he was arrested by the Provost Marshal, 11th Corps, Army of the Potomac, and charged with belonging to the Confederate Army. His name appeared as "Eliyah Hutchinson." He also appears on a roster of Prisoners of War

(POW) at Old Capital Prison in Washington, D.C. who had been exchanged, released, or had died during the month of October 1862. From the Old Capitol Prison in Washington, D.C. he was transferred to Fortress Monroe.

At this time in the war, according to his Confederate Service Record, he also appeared on a list of Prisoners of War, paroled until regularly exchanged and delivered at Aiken's Landing 2 November 1862. Aiken's Landing (now Varina) is in Virginia, along the James River. On 22 July, an agreement was made between the Confederate and the Union governments on how to handle the general exchange, known as the Dix-Hill Cartel. Initially, at the beginning of the war, President Lincoln did not want to negotiate with the Confederates, whom they called "Rebels," because he did not believe in giving them recognition, which included any type of prisoner exchange. President Lincoln and public opinion was very content with this deal—that is, until over 1,000 Union prisoners were captured at the First Battle of Bull Run.

Apparently, the exchange of prisoners was a very time-consuming process. There were two POW sites in Virginia: one at Aiken's Landing, and one at Dutch Gap. The agreement included stipulations for exchanging civilians, disloyal citizens, families of soldiers, and civilian employees. A scale of equivalents was designed for management of exchange, such as that a captain would be equivalent to fifteen privates. Thankfully, the Union-Confederate prisoner exchange system worked for our Elijah, as General Grant reviewed this system in 1864 and made modifications. President Lincoln had directed General Grant to stop exchanging captured prisoners because the Confederates were returning to the battlefields and the Union prisoners were often in poor medical condition, which resulted in handicapped soldiers. In *The Longest Night*, historian David J. Eicher states that the "Union Army paroled or exchanged 329,963 Confederate prisoners of war, while the Confederacy paroled or exchanged about 152,015 Union prisoners of war," but unfortunately he does not disclose where he found those numbers.[18]

By this time, both armies were settling in for the winter of 1862–1863; winter quarters were set up in various places, which was also dependent upon finding forage for the animals. From 1 December 1862 through 26 January 1863, Company K members served as message runners for General Jackson, both personally and for his staff. The entire regiment, including the 6th Virginia, was under the direct command of Colonel Flournoy and Lt. Colonel John Shack Green. Major Cabell E. Flournoy departed winter quarters and marched from a point near Mount Crawford North, stopping five miles from New Market. He was forced to make camp about a mile from Mount Jackson due to a major snow storm. On 27 January 1863, there was another major snowstorm.[10]

Elijah was still a prisoner during this time period, and he appears on the 12 December Muster roll as absent and last paid by Carter through 1 July 1862. His record shows that on 30 December 1862, he was paid from 2 July 1862–30 December 1862 the amount of $138.12. I am not sure who received his monies, as he was still a Prisoner of War at Aiken's Landing, Virginia. As of 13 December 1862, Company K was in Fredericksburg, Virginia with only sixty-five men left in the group.[10]

Elijah's Service record shows that he was finally released in a prisoner exchange on 24 February 1863 and he returned to his Company K for duty on the same day. He was present for Muster in February 1863, and on 2 March he was paid near Guinea Station Depot a tidy sum of $158.12 for clothing and the use and risk of horse.

CHAPTER 5:
Elijah Returns From His POW Experience

As Elijah was now safe and back in action, he and the company made camp a mile below Woodstock, Virginia in Shenandoah County on 15 March 1863. On 19 March, the Company moved their camp to Front Royal, approximately twenty-four miles from Woodstock. On 3 April, much merriment was had, as the company had a snowball fight, where Lt. John H Matthews breaking his arm. When I read about the big snowball fight, I laughed so hard. On 21 April, Major Flournoy was the senior officer in command. The regiment broke camp and met up with General Grumble Jones' brigade in Brock's Gap. On 22 April, the Brigade receives a new Commanding Officer, as Lt. Colonel John Shack Green resumes charge of the Brigade.[10]

I have not been able to find out when Elijah got a new horse, but logical conclusions tell me that when he went home, after he was returned from capture, he brought back another one of his mares. After all, what good is a cavalryman without a horse? It is quite interesting how the Confederates resupplied their armies with horses. The horses had to be well-trained and disciplined in order to be successful in a battle, and the training was intense. The officers usually had more than one horse, just in case a horse was shot our from under them in the heat of battle; however, for the enlisted men, like Elijah, there was one horse, which they brought from home. It would be logical that the Armies purchased and trained horses from farmers who raised them. Horses had to be fed and brushed daily and bedded down. When men lost their horses, at least in the Confederacy, the government reimbursed men for loss of the horse, and essentially paid the men rent for their horse. In looking at Elijah's service record, you can see when he was paid for the use of his horse. In all of the sadness of the war, I think the horses got the short end of the stick.

West Virginia was my next place of a great adventure, and of course, the places I needed to find Elijah were definitely off the beaten path; I'm very thankful that I chose to get a Jeep for my explorations. I love maps and geography, so I knew there were many high mountains and I had in the past driven through the nice interstates with regular places to stop, get some gas, and find real restrooms. Well, in order to really find Elijah, I knew I had to bite the bullet and follow his route. I absolutely do not like tiny roads with steep hills, many switchbacks and no guardrails.

I had experienced that a few years back when Alex, my son, and I were driving around France and he convinced me to take a shortcut through the Alps. You might ask what I was doing driving in the Alps, but all he had wanted for his high-school graduation gift was to drive around France for three weeks, and I just couldn't say no to such an adventure. To say the least, that was an experience, especially when the rented car decided to turn off while we were going down a steep, tiny, winding small mountain road. That experience definitely left a bad taste for mountainous roads, which after six years still has not dissipated. So, that being said, I was not exactly filled with exuberance at the idea of driving over the mountains. Personally, I'd much rather walk! But I had no choice but to face my fears, which is what everyone says to do. Besides, how else could I find Elijah? I knew my Jeep had four-wheel drive and special gears to prevent speeding down steep mountains, so I was ready…or so I thought.

West Virginia Campaign (April 1863)

We were in great spirits as we began this leg of our adventure. The sun was shining, which is always a great sign, and the temperature was very pleasant. Things were going fine as we tootled along the breathtaking road to our next

Rowlesburg, WV. Photo by G. Lindner

battle site: Rowlesburg, West Virginia, which included driving through a lovely valley, where there were majestic wind turbines on the hills and beautiful green fields. At one point, we both saw a majestic hawk fly over our Jeep, up-close and personal. The hooked beak was amazing, and for a split second, the bird and I looked into each other's soul. What would possess a bird to nearly land on the top of a moving car? Strange. The road was nice and wide, until we found our next road. As we departed from the interstate, I knew we were taking the roads that Elijah rode on his horse; and every time I thought about this (which was quite often) I couldn't imagine how he did it back in the day, especially with no radio to listen to!

The greatest adventure yet, I believe, is when Elijah was near Greenland Gap, Virginia, which is in present-day West Virginia. Springtime in the West Virginia Mountains brings a lot of rain. As the 1863 rainy season approached, Elijah and his group set out for the western part of Virginia with a mission to prevent the Federals from taking natural resources. In Petersburg, West Virginia, along the South Branch of the Shenandoah River on 24 April 1863, they were looking for a place to cross the river. The river was flowing very high, and once again, the 6th Virginia Cavalry had been chosen to lead the group across the dangerous waters.[10] Apparently, many locals placed themselves at various parts of the river to help them cross. Chaplain Davis rode out to the middle of the river and prayed for every man's safe passage as they forded the river. On 25 April, at Greenland Gap, they encountered eighty-three Union troops from the 23rd Illinois Regiment, commanded by Captain Martin Wallace. The 6th Virginia Cavalry set fire to the log church, where the Federals had taken shelter, causing them to surrender. Surgeon James S. Lewis was the only 6th Virginia Cavalry casualty.[10]

There are some great stories out of this battle, two primary source documents, which are below, told of a great adventure.

The Rebellion Record: A Diary of American Events, with Documents, Narratives, Illustrative Incidents, Poetry Etc.

Frank Moore, ed. Vol. 6. New York: G. P. Putnam, 1863.

A fight took place at Greenland Gap, Va., between a detachment of Union troops, under the command of Captain Wallace, of the Twenty-third Illinois, and a numerically superior body of rebels, under General William E. Jones. The contests lasted nearly two hours, the rebels making three desperate charges, but were repulsed on each occasion with heavy Loss. The rebel killed and wounded outnumbered the whole Union force.

Doc. 176.

The Fight at Greenland Gap, Virginia General Kelley's Dispatch. Greenland Gap, Harding [sic] County, Va., April 28, 1863.

To Lieutenant-Colonel Cheeseborough, A. A. G.

The affair at this place, on Saturday, was one of the most gallant since the opening of the war. Greenland Gap is a pass through the Knobley Mountain, only wide enough for the road and a small mountain stream. This gap was guarded by Union Captain Wallace (with a detachment of company G, Twenty-third Illinois regiment, and a small detachment of company H, Thirteenth Virginia infantry, Captain Smith, in all between seventy and eighty men).

Captain Wallace occupied a large church at the west end of and near the mouth of the gap, and Captain Smith held a log-house about a hundred yards distant, both positions commanding the gap. Jones was compelled to capture or dislodge the little band before he could pass.

*His troops made three gallant charges, but were each time
repulsed with great loss, especially of officers. The fight
commenced at five P. M., and lasted till after dark. The
rebels, availing themselves of the darkness, approached
and fired the church, but the gallant Irish boys would
not even then surrender till the burning roof fell in.
The killed and wounded of the rebels outnumbered our
whole force engaged. Five of the officers out of the eight
commanding the leading battalion, which made the first
charge, were either killed or wounded, among the latter
Colonel Dulany, commanding. Captains Wallace and
Smith had only two men killed and four wounded. I
counted, to-day, eighteen dead horses with musket-range.
I most earnestly request the Major-General Commanding to apply to the Secretary of War to have every officer,
non-commissioned officer and private engaged in the
fight presented with a medal, in recognition of the gallantry displayed.*

*B. F. Kelley,
Union Brigadier-General* [19]

The excitement was certainly not over yet! The Brigade,
now under the command of Brigadier General William T.
"Grumble" Jones, numbered 3,500 men when they left Rockingham County on 21 April 1863. It met resistance at Greenland Gap, Virginia on 25 April from the 23rd Illinois Regiment
and for four hours, both sides had combat action. They camped
that night at Red House (the intersection of US 219 and US
50). On 26 April 1863, at 2 p.m., the regiment finally reached

the Baltimore & Ohio Railroad Bridge, across the Cheat River, near Rowlesburg, Virginia (soon to be West Virginia).[10]

The next day, the 6th Cavalry went with other troops to destroy the wood-and-iron bridge, which crossed the Cheat River, along with the iron bridge that crossed Tray Run in Rowlesburg, Virginia (which is now West Virginia).[10] Our journey to relive this battle was nearly complete. Finally, after driving along National Route 50, which had no line in the pavement, and often no guardrail, we reached our destination road. I might add that a truck going too fast around one of the switchbacks nearly knocked me off the road. But, instead of being afraid, I continued along our path. When I pulled over and got out of the car, I couldn't help but wonder how in the heck was there a battle fought here, in the middle of mountains and streams. The town is very charming and people live up in the hills. This tiny town should definitely be on the top ten best places to visit in the country.

Rowlesburg, officially established in 1858, is on the National Register of Historic Places. Elijah and his cavalry soon realize that Union soldiers occupied this small town nestled in the Cheat Valley, along the Cheat River. The story has it that the B & O Railroad, which went through this town, was extremely important to President Lincoln's West Virginia campaign. However, in 1861, the Union had few troops stationed here, so when the Confederate cavalry arrived in April 1863 they found themselves facing many angry townies, along with a few Federal soldiers.[20]

Only 250 Federal troops were stationed at Rowlesburg on the Northwestern Turnpike, now US 50. However, the initial Confederate assault was turned back by this small force because

Rowlesburg, WV. Photo by G. Lindner

Union armed civilians came out to assist in the fighting and even brought a cannon. Brigadier General Jones then moved the rest of his brigade two miles west to Macomber, where the River Road (now WV 72) connected Rowlesburg to the Northwestern Turnpike.[20] The 6th Virginia Cavalry attacked Union pickets on the north flanks to squeeze the defenders of Rowlesburg. Less than a mile from town, a log barricade held them up and Federal troops opened fire. Captain Green then ordered the 6th Cavalry to fall back—a decision which so infuriated Jones that he would initiate court-martial proceedings against Captain Green.[10]

Three assaults failed to dislodge the Federals, who were aided by twenty armed civilians. As the two sides fought along the River Road, it was very difficult for the cavalry to make any headway in the battle; the hills were steep, and those poor horses were sliding down the hillsides. The Confederates had great difficulty overtaking their opponents, who were solidly entrenched in their hillside positions. They could not be overtaken. They charged the 6th Virginia Cavalry, who, by this time in the action, had dismounted their horses and run. In the end, the 6th Cavalry lost the battle and General Jones pulled back to the Turnpike, then headed west. General Jones reported disobedience charges against Lt. Col. Green, his reason being that Green "allowed himself to be stopped by less than 20 men." However, on 17 September 1863, a Court Martial acquitted Lt. Col. Green. Rowlesburg was the only place in western Virginia to survive this Confederate campaign, and the rail bridge over the Cheat River remained intact.[21] As I stood there on the bridge, looking at the battle site, those hills were very steep; I couldn't even imagine why the Confederates thought this battle plan was a good idea.

Departing this very exciting battle site, the 6th Cavalry led the entire regiment as they crossed the suspension bridge above the Monongahela River, on the way to Morgantown, Virginia (later West Virginia) on 28 April 1863. Upon passing through, the center of the bridge shifted down, leaving the bridge suspended only by cables, hanging sixty feet in the air looking down to the rocky gorge below. As they successfully crossed the bridge, one can only imagine the fear. They did not destroy the bridge, hoping the Union troops would finish off the bridge as they chased the Cavalry across, continuing their march by night to Fairmont, Virginia (later West Virginia).

On 29 April, the morning was foggy in Fairmont, and Union sharpshooters were all around, capturing 268 6th Virginia Cavalry members as prisoners. But they immediately released the men. After the release ceremony, the train brought Union cannons and reinforcements and broke out in fighting for a second time. 6th Virginia captured a cannon and the 12th Virginia appeared; because of this, the Union troops made way quickly to the train and departed the area. Three men from 6th Virginia were wounded, but no one died. Next, the 6th Cavalry decided to blow up the Bridge.[10]

In this adventure, I came across an account of this battle as well, and wanted to share the story, written just days after the Confederates captured Fairmont.

Confederates Capture Fairmont (Virginia)
Wheeling Daily Intelligencer
May 5, 1863

The Battle Of Fairmont
Three Hours Desperate Fighting!
300 Unionists Against 6,000 Rebels.
Fairmont, Va., May 4, 1863.

Editors Intelligencer:

The rebel raid into West Virginia has come and gone. The smoke of battle has drifted away, and the thousand rumors have given place to well determined facts. I propose to describe briefly what I understand to be the route taken by the raiders after entering our lines until they escaped beyond them, and, with as much detail as time will permit, the engagement at this place.

It appears that on Friday and Saturday, the 24th and 25th results, the rebels, having driven our small forces from Beverly and Philippi back to Grafton, crossed the railroad at several points between Grafton and Rowles-

*burg, and went to Kingwood, in Preston county, thence to
Morgantown, which place they reached on Monday at 2
P. M. Tuesday morning they left Morgantown and came
up on the east bank of the river to within seven or eight
miles of this place, where they were met by another body,
which crossed the railroad subsequently. The whole force
then returned to Morgantown, crossed the river, spread
out over the country, taking every good horse they could
find, and concentrated here on Wednesday morning. They
crossed Buffalo Creek - which flows from the west and
enters the river a mile below town - at Barracksville, and
approached town on the Mannington pike. The first positive information of their number and whereabouts was
received from Morgantown on Monday evening. Their
number was estimated by a gentleman who witnessed
their entre, at 5,000. Before this news came, and whilst
all was vague rumor and perplexing uncertainty, many of
our fighting men whom we relied upon as certain to die
in "the last ditch" if die they must, performed "a grand
strategical [sic] movement" and "fell back" to a new "base
of operations" at Cameron, Moundsville, Wheeling, and
various other points in Ohio and Pennsylvania. Those
whose lips retained the crimson hue of natural life, and
whose knees did not quake like Caesar's with the ague
in Spain, remained and busied themselves in hunting
up arms and in making every effort to defend the place
against the impending assault. A delegation went to
Mannington and returned on Tuesday morning with two
companies of militia and as many guns as were fit for use.
The whole defensive force consisted of only 300 men, made*

up of companies D and F, 106th N. Y. Vols. - 105 men; two companies of the 176th Virginia militia - 117 men; 38 men of company A, 6th Va. a few of company N, 6th Virginia, and about 40 citizen soldiers.

The rebel army was commanded by Gen. Wm. E. Jones, and consisted, according to his statement, of 7 regiments of cavalry, 1 regiment of mounted infantry and 300 mounted sharp shooters, in all 6,000 men, many of them being of the celebrated Ashby's cavalry.

Wednesday morning dawned wet and foggy; our scouts came dashing in and reported the enemy approaching only two or three miles off. One company of militia and most of the armed citizens went out on the hills to meet him. About eight o'clock picket firing commenced and was kept up briskly for half an hour. The enemy finding we were posted on the hills prepared to rake him severely as he came down the pike along Coal Run, sent a heavy force on the hills to drive us off. In this they succeeded after several of them had been summarially [sic] unhorsed. The men from the hills retreated, some to the main force, near the railroad bridge, a mile above town, and some to the Palatine end of the Suspension Bridge. The latter made a gallant stand and resisted the crossing for nearly an hour. They took shelter in a Foundry and fired from the windows upon the rebel sharpshooters, who dismounted and took positions in vacant houses, behind fences, stables and whatever else would conceal their cowardly carcass from our unerring aim. Thus was the unequal contest continued until one man, named Coffman, from Bingamon, was fatally wounded, and all but five or six had straggled off. The remainder ceased firing and each one took care of himself as best he could. When the firing ceased the rebels sent over a flag of truce to demand a surrender, but to their astonishment they found no one to receive it. They then hastily replaced the plank which had been removed from the bridge, and crossed over to the number of nearly a thousand, and pushed on up to get in the rear of our men at the Railroad Bridge.

While the fight at the suspension bridge was going on the rebels disposed their main force for attack at the upper bridge. Our force in defence [sic] of the railroad bridge, now about 275, had taken up a position half a mile northwest of the bridge and within gunshot of the road leading to Pruntytown. As the rebel cavalry dashed along this road in order to reach the river above the bridge, they were exposed to a raking and destructive fire, which unhorsed ten or twelve of them. Having crossed at the suspension bridge and occupied the heights at the eastern end of the railroad bridge and gained the river above, they had our men completely surrounded. From his position on the heights to the rear and immediately overlooking the spartan band, the commanding General called out, "Why the h-ll don't you surrender?" Our boys send back a defiant response, when he immediately commanded his men to "Rally." Then began of the most desperate and unequal contests of this or any other war. For some time the rattle of musketry was incessant. Our men were in open meadows, protected somewhat from the fire in front by ravines, but exposed to the rebel sharpshooters behind *rocks and trees on the right bank of the river. Inch by inch were we forced back to within two hundred yards of the bridge, all the time coolly loading and firing for the most part after deliberate aim at the cowardly rebels, who, notwithstanding they had twenty to our one, fought Indian fashion from behind whatever would conceal them. Finding further resistance utterly hopeless and just as the rebel cavalry were ready for a grand charge, which must have resulted in the total destruction of the gallant little band, a white flag was raised from a house near by and the firing ceased.*

Scarcely had the formalities of the capitulation been completed when two pieces of ordnance from Mulligan's command at Grafton opened on them from the opposite side of the river. They then double quicked the prisoners off the field and placed them in the Court House, where they were paroled about 9 o'clock at night. The rebels on the left bank of the river were soon shelled out of range, but those on the same side as the battery made a desperate effort to tear up the road in the rear of the battery to prevent its return. They took up one or more rails and piled several cords of wood on the track, but after a sharp engagement they were driven off by eighty men of Company B, 106 New York, and a few rounds from the cannon. While the train bearing the battery was behind the hill protecting itself from being cut off and captured, the rebels commenced the destruction of the Railroad bridge which was doubtless the finest structure of the kind in the United States. It was made of iron, supported by four piers of massive stonework and was about nine hundred feet long.

The iron work was above the piers and was supported by tubular columns of cast iron. In these hollow columns, they poured kegs of powder which they had brought along for the purpose, and in this way, the noble structure was blown from the piers into the river. The whole cost of its erection was $496,000, two thirds of which was expended in getting the piers above the high water mark owing to the great depth of water and mud above the solid rock. The destruction of this bridge is one of the most serious losses this Railroad has sustained during the war. Months must elapse before even a temporary bridge can be erected.

The battle we have endeavored to describe, was fought on Wednesday, April 29th, and was in many respects the most remarkable in the annals of warfare. The great disparity in the numbers engaged; the obstinate, determined resistance made by the Unionists; the length of time they held out; and, stranger still, only one killed and four wounded on our side, while the rebel loss, according to their own admission, was fifty to sixty. Indeed, Gen. Jones told Captain Chamberlin that we had killed and disabled about a hundred of his men.

He, as well as the rebel soldie[r]s, complimented us on the gallantry with which we maintained our various positions. Where all who took up arms did so well, it would be invidious to particularize indizidual [sic] acts of heroism.

Capt. Chamberlin, of Co. F, 106th N. Y. Vols., had command of the post. Major Parish, of the militia, and each citizen soldier commanded himself, and as many more as would obey him.

Every store in town was robbed of everything the thieves fancied. The home rebels pointed out the private property they wanted destroyed, and it was done. A valuable stem saw mill, belon[g]ing to J. N. Cromwell & Co., was burned. The National printing office was destroyed because it has been uncompromisingly Union, while the butternut concern in Morgantown was uninjured because, as the traitors said, it was on their side and was devoted to their cause. The law and private libraries of Gov. Peirpont were carried into the street in front of his office and burned; every horse in town and the surrounding country was taken. At least five hundred horses were taken out of Marion county alone.

Fortunately, the Union men had moved their horses out of the neighborhood, while the Secesh relied upon their opposition to the Government, which has always protected them, for security. Hence in the loss of horses they are by far the greater sufferers, as the raiders were no respecters of persons in making their selections. Some men who have all along been very desirous to get their "rights," have had a little foretaste of what their rights are in the estimation of traitors. The miserable Copperheads who have been opposing the war, and growling about taxes, have lost more by the men whose rights they are so jealous of than the Government expects them to pay as taxes for the next ten years.

Aside from the loss of property, we have no doubt this raid will have a good effect, it will open the eyes of the people and of the Government to the necessity of adopting far more rigid measures with home rebels, who act as spies, furnishing the information which enable these raids to successfully enter and escape from our lines. We used to hear a great deal about confiscating their property and leaving them as poor as a church mouse; but as far as our observation extends, the rebels in West Virginia are getting rich by the war.

Let us for the future take prompt and effective measures for the removal of every disloyal person, male and female, old and young, south of our State and military lines. What else can be done with the women who fired from houses on our soldiers as they were retreating through town the other day, who waved handkerchiefs and cheered the thieves and robbers as they came into town, and jeered and laughed at our gallant boys as they were marched prisoners of war into town from a hard fought battle field? What should be done with rebel men and boys who spent the day in riding about the streets with the rebels, pointing out private property which they wished destroyed? They are not as poor as church mice, for they can store up cart loads of sweet cakes and pies several days before the rebels come in. You may ask, were all these things done? Certainly they were; yet the rebels here have the unblushing impudence to boast of having saved the whole town from being burned to the ground! If something is not soon done with these home rebels, companies will be organized who will undertake to dispose of them in a way that may be deemed rather more hempish than red tapish. [22]

Elijah was definitely on a mission with the 6th Virginia in the forefront of the action! On 30 April 1863, the Brigade took Bridgeport, Virginia (now in West Virginia). The 6th Cavalry provided sharpshooting and picket duty, while the brigade seized the town and destroyed the railroad trestle. The brigade marched through the mountains and was attacked by snipers, called the "Swamp Dragons," using guerilla warfare for the Union against Confederates. Bridgeport, located in Harrison County, was officially chartered in 1816, but not incorporated until 1887.[10] In 1856, the Baltimore and Ohio Railroad ran through the town, which then enabled the ranchers to transport their cattle by rail to market. As fate would have it, we stayed the night in Bridgeport, which today is a lovely, sprawled out, very clean little city with a brand new hospital, a Sheetz gas station, and an Outback Restaurant.

As we looked at the map, we continued to follow the Jones-Imboden Civil War Road and planned our next day's drive to Burning Springs. You too can follow this road, although you may want to allow two days for the journey. I dreaded more winding roads and kept wishing that we could go as the hawk flies, because the surface roads take much longer to get there, as they are not direct. The drive along the Little Kanawha River was absolutely beautiful: the flowers were blooming, and the river was peacefully flowing, but the roads were tiny and very close to the River. Even so, I was filled with anticipation, as I was excited to see this very important site in the West Virginia campaign.

After the Confederates left Bridgeport on 9 May 1863, just eight miles from the Ohio River on the little Kanawha River, the 6th Virginia had a great deal of action in Burning

Little Kanawha River, Burning Springs, WV. Photo by G. Lindner

Springs, Wirt County, Virginia (now West Virginia). The Brigade arrived at Oiltown, Virginia (the name Jones called Burning Springs).[10] There were a huge number of oil reserves here, which were originally drilled for petroleum, and later kerosene. During the Civil War, Burning Springs was the second largest operating oil well in the United States, with the first being in Titusville, Pennsylvania, which also produced kerosene. The first oil wells had been discovered only a few years before in 1860; and in the beginning, they produced one hundred barrels of oil a day. Before the war, there were over 700 oil leases that had been applied for in order to drill the rich oil.[23] Most of the oil wells were on land which was owned by local citizens, who legally leased the oil wells; however the Federal Government confiscated these oil wells for lighting and military equipment grease.[24]

The boys were definitely having some Saturday night fun blowing up the oil barrels. Brigadier General Jones said that the property had been taken control of by the Federal Government,

Rathbone Well, Burning Springs, WV. Photo by G. Lindner

so they ignited 300,000 barrels of oil, which had been loaded on the boats. Then, they went on to capture the towns of West Union and Cairo. Along the way, they burned five bridges and disabled a railroad tunnel.[10] (In my research, I found various numbers of barrels that the Confederates burned; however the number I used was provided from the information at the actual site of the Rathbone Well in Burning Springs.)

General Jones then ordered his troops to burn all the oil equipment (derricks, storage barrels and tanks, pumps, and wagons). Since the barrels had already been loaded on barges, the Little Kanawha River caught on fire and filled the air.[10] (Note: the source claims that 150,000 barrels of oil were burned, but Northern sources put the number at 300,000). Protecting the oil well was none other than Union Colonel Rathbone of the 11th West Virginia Infantry. No citizens were harmed— perhaps because they had three hours' advance warning, and fled west toward Parkersburg. Five Confederate soldiers died by accidental explosion. The estimated damage of $40 million makes Burning Springs the most destructive raid on northern industry of the war.[25] Eyewitnesses reported, "The burnings turned Little Kanawha River into a sheet of fire." Apparently, there were several thousand barrels of whiskey that they purposefully torched. There were also several nearby houses that were incinerated including the Chicago House, which was the local house of ill repute.[26] The 6th Virginia Cavalry had fewer than twelve casualties.[10]

Next, the 6th Cavalry joined General Imboden's cavalry at Summersville, where they captured 28 wagons, 170 mules, and some more livestock. Jones' brigade passed through Greenbrier County, resting at White Sulphur Springs on 17 May at the "Old White." They later camped near Mount Crawford in Rockingham on 21 May. Jones estimated that about thirty of the enemy's men were killed and 700 prisoners taken. He added about 400 new recruits, an artillery piece, 1,000 head of cattle, and 1,200 horses. His men destroyed sixteen bridges, an oil field, many boats, and rolling rail stock.[10]

I really enjoyed my adventure to this small, out-of-the-way town. The park was very clean, nature-friendly, and not artificially inflated as a glitzy tourist trap; however if you plan on visiting, there are very few public buildings or bathrooms! I find it very interesting that still today, much about what happened in Burning Springs is still being researched and new information surfacing. I found a very informative article, written in 2014 by Dave McKain, who also happens to be the Chairman of the Civil War Roundtable in Burning Springs, and I look forward to watching a documentary that was released in early Spring 2014. According to Dave McKain, Director of the Oil and Gas Museum in Burning Springs,

"We have acquired, since we published "Where It All Began" (1994), many new pieces of information about what went on there during the Civil War. This new information is important in that it helps us understand a large piece of the

West Virginia oil industry and Civil War history, because it helps explain how important the Confederate guerilla activity was in hurting the Union war effort in this area. This also affected the national war effort because the activity at Burning Springs was a microcosm of the guerilla war effort across the state along the strategically critical B&O railroad and south."[23]

May was definitely an active month for Elijah and his cavalry. "Elijah Hutchison, Private, Company K, 6 Virginia Cavalry" appears on a receipt roll for clothing for 234 Qrs on 21 May 1863. As you recall, the 6th Virginia had destroyed the Baltimore and Ohio Railroad Bridge earlier in a raid; however, by 22 May, as the Cavalry returns to Mount Crawford, the bridge had completely been restored and was functional. Of the earlier raid, John Opie, a 6th Virginia Cavalry soldier said, "It was a fruitless and unimportant raid."

On 23 May at McCoy's Ferry, the entire 6th Virginia Cavalry crossed the South Fork of the Shenandoah River and destroyed the Manassas Gap Railroad (on present-day U.S. Route 29) in the Shenandoah Valley. When the Cavalry came to the bridge at Front Royal over the North Forks, they rapidly crossed the burning bridge over the Shenandoah River. One can only imagine the speed at which they were riding those horses. After they crossed at Front Royal, some of the 6th Cavalry attacked the Federal pickets on guard, and they continued to ride three more miles north to Cedarville, Virginia (also known as Ninevah) to capture some artillery. Sadly, Company Commander George A. Baxter was killed in the skirmish at Cedarville. The Federal Army had made a stand here.[10]

On 27 May, Brigadier General Jones conducted a meeting with the purpose of reviewing the actions of Lt. Colonel Green and Major Flournoy. Many interviews with the men revealed they liked Lt. Colonel Green personally, but felt that he was not effective in his leadership role. The end result was his replacement by Colonel Julien Harrison. At the end of May, the 6th Virginia Cavalry broke camp and marched to join General J. E. B. Stuart in Culpeper County. However, they encountered a delay near Brown's Gap in northwestern Albemarle County as they looked for deserters.[10] Just an aside, Brown's Gap, in the Blue Ridge Mountains, has an interesting name, as it is only known as Brown's Gap on the East side; however on the West side it is known as Madison's Gap.[27]

The Battle of Brandy Station (June 1863)
The waiting between Chancellorsville and Gettysburg

While we were looking for Brandy Station, where the ceremonial reviews were being held, we had a bit of an adventure. Due to a month of heavy snows, and then buckets of rain, the ground was very soft. In Virginia, all the road signs are literally placed where the adventure happened, so you have to be prepared to immediately pull off the road and hope no one is behind you as you flicker your turn signal for a moment. It was a very cold Saturday when we ventured to the Brandy Station Battlefield, on our way to check out Culpeper. We saw a wonderful sign and, per usual, I pulled off the side of the road into nice, red, very mushy mud, which was much deeper than it looked. Needless to say, I didn't get a look at that sign, but I am always very thankful for four-wheel drive on my Jeep, which I had just washed and waxed—at this point, it was now a huge muddy mess. The Jeep was covered with mud. As I unstuck the car, it flung mud every which direction—even on the windshield! With all that excitement, we moved onto the next wonderful find, which was the hill that the 6th Cavalry charged up to set up General J. E. B. Stuart's headquarters. It was really cool standing there once again, where Elijah had been. I didn't even mind that it was 16 degrees out and the winds were whipping across the hill. I was so enamored by the view that I am sharing photos of both directions from where I was standing, and, of course, my very muddy Jeep.

As June began, the 6th Virginia met up with General J. E. B. Stuart and took part in a ceremonial Grand Review of the troops at Brandy Station, Virginia. Confederate General Robert E. Lee, commander of The Army of Northern Virginia, conducted another review on 8 June.[10]

The next day, Elijah would see a huge battle of engagement

Confederate Headquarters, Brandy Station Battlefield, VA. My very muddy adventure jeep is sitting on the hillside. Photo by G. Lindner

at the Battle of Brandy Station. Union General John Buford and his 1st Cavalry Division started the process of crossing Beverly Ford at the Rappahannock River at 4:30 a.m., before daybreak. Elijah definitely saw some excitement here, as he and the 6th Virginia Cavalry protected this area along with Captain Bruce Gibson's Company A. The Union 1st Cavalry Division initially attacked the Confederate Company A, which briefly halted the 1st Cavalry. Then Company A swiftly rode to the main body of the Confederate regiment, which was several miles away near St. James Church at the Gee House. Though they found horses had been unsaddled and were grazing in the fresh grass, Confederate 6th Virginia Major Flournoy quickly got 150 of his men mounted and ready to go, racing up Beverly Ford Road, on the right side of the road. The 7th Virginia was on the left side of the road and the 6th Virginia was on the right side, traveling full speed, attacking the Federals in the woods.[10]

It was a difficult battle because the Confederates were unable to contain the Federals for a long time. As Buford continued to advance his division, the 6th Cavalry held firm, while the baggage was safely removed back to St. James Church. Turning left, they united with General Wade Hampton's Brigade and, later that day, the 6th Virginia Cavalry very quickly made their way from St. James Church to Fleetwood, as the two sides attacked and counter-attacked.[10] Federal troops climbed the hill on one side, while Confederates came up the hill on the other side. Continuous charges, and counter-charges occurred throughout this very desperate day. The Confederates were successful in hand-to-hand fighting, and captured a section of artillery before they were driven back by the Federals. This ten-hour engagement must have been grueling for both sides.[28]

This Battle of Brandy Station, which took place on Fleetwood Hill, is believed to have been the largest Civil War battle that was fought between mostly cavalry forces. Historians argue that this was a tactical draw, but that both cavalries demonstrated the same skill level of combat capabilities. However, when it was all said and done, the 6th Virginia casualties included 5 dead, 25 wounded (some mortally, but that number is not given) and 25 prisoners.[28]

The Gettysburg Campaign Begins (June 1863)
Battle of Upperville

A few days later, on 19 June, the 6th Virginia was at Pot House, Virginia. Pot House was a small, unincorporated community (present-day Leithtown), located between Middleburg and Union (which is present-day Unison), where the roads of Foxcroft, Pot House, and Mountville intersect. Yup, Elijah is back at his favorite Mountville intersection. The situation was different, though, because he didn't get captured again, nor did he lose a horse. There were shots volleyed back and forth, which led to the Battle of Upperville on 21 June.[10]

Tucked behind a stone fence, the 6th Virginia covered the retreat for the wagon train and the rest of the cavalry to safely escape to Ashby's Gap.[10] At the Battle of Upperville, General Robert E. Lee's army was concentrated just west of Upperville in Loudoun County, Virginia, and General J. E. B. Stuart's cavalry was screening them from Union General Pleasanton's cavalry. When Pleasanton attacked the morning of 21 June 1863, General J. E. B. Stuart fought with delaying actions

Upperville, VA. Photo by G. Lindner

to get his men safely to Upperville. Union Brigadier General John Buford's brigade led the assault on Upperville while the balance of the Union forces assaulted Ashby's Gap (Route 50 today).[29] Elijah and the 6th Virginia Cavalry was in Upperville, along with Stuart's supply wagons. Pleasanton eventually withdrew, still not knowing that Lee's army was already crossing the Potomac into Maryland and eventually into Pennsylvania. When it was all over, the 6th Virginia counted one dead and ten wounded.[10]

Once again, camp was set up in Berryville, Virginia on 28 June 1863, about twenty-one miles from Ashby's Gap. General J. E. B. Stuart did not take the 6th Virginia Cavalry with him on his ride around the Federal Army, as he took the rest of his division to the famous offensive battle in Gettysburg, Pennsylvania. Confederate General Robert E. Lee had ordered the 6th Virginia Cavalry and all the rest of the Brigades left behind to join him in Gettysburg; however, General Stuart stopped to look for shoes and supplies for his men instead of going directly to meet General Lee in Gettysburg, as ordered.

The famous Cashtown Inn, reputed to be actively haunted, and was also shown in the movie Gettysburg, *located in Cashtown, PA. Photo by G. Lindner*

The late arrival of General Stuart definitely changed the course of events significantly for the Confederates at the Battle of Gettysburg.[10]

The March to Gettysburg (July 1863)

General Stuart took his group north to Gettysburg by way of Martinsburg, West Virginia, crossing the Potomac River at Williamsport, Maryland, and continuing through Chambersburg, Pennsylvania and Cashtown, Pennsylvania on 3 July. Cashtown, Pennsylvania is the site of the famed Cashtown Inn and Restaurant, which is said to be haunted according to visitors who stay the night. I was so excited as I stood in front of the building, knowing that Elijah had walked here. As we went inside, I could smell the history, and at one point, I felt a warm breath across my face. Was I connecting with the past? Here, on 3 July 1863 at 1 p.m., the 6th Virginia Cavalry received orders to march southwards toward Fairfield, Pennsylvania, following the Fairfield-Orrtanna Road. The gunshots and cannonballs could be easily heard from the Battle of Gettysburg, about eight miles to the east, as the

The Inside parlor of The Cashtown Inn, the building that the 6th Virginia Cavalry rode past on their way to meet General Robert E. Lee at Gettysburg, Pennsylvania. Photo by G. Lindner

heavy fighting took place. This battle was the turning point of the Eastern Theater of War, as this would be the last attempt that General Lee and his Confederate Army would launch in the attempt to bring the war to the North. They would then turn and march to Washington, D.C. for their final battle. The 6th Virginia did not make it to Gettysburg.[10]

The Battle of Fairfield (July 1863)

I can only imagine the chaos that ensued on this third day of July 1863, because when I drove this route along the Fairfield-Orrtanna Road, it was hilly, and the road wasn't very wide. At this time of year back then, there would have been mud from the waters flowing from the rivers. Alongside the road, Confederate wagons sped rapidly past Elijah's group as they made haste in their approach from the south. The Battle of Fairfield, Pennsylvania was about to take place in a very large cornfield, located in an open, remote countryside surrounded by mountains.

Fairfield, PA. Photo by G. Lindner

When we found the battle sign, we pulled into the ditch on the side of the road and got out of the Jeep. Why would anyone fight a battle in an open field? There were no trees, only mountains off in the distance and a very eerie silence, perhaps in respect to the sacred battlefield.

Union Major Samuel H. Starr's 6th U.S. Cavalry Regiment had been ordered to capture all wagons that were travelling in the countryside with the mission of gathering food and clothing for Confederate soldiers. When General J. E. B. Stuart rode around the Union army just before the Battle of Gettysburg, he left Grumble Jones' brigade (with Elijah's 6th Virginia) behind to guard the Hagerstown Road and ensure a supply line and escape route.[10] The 7th Virginia Cavalry led the way, with the 6th Virginia Cavalry following immediately behind.

Major Starr and the 6th U.S. Cavalry learned that the Confederate wagon train was heading toward Cashtown. Confederate General Grumble T. Jones ordered the 7th Cavalry to charge by themselves without reinforcements. This decision had not been well-thought out, because unbeknownst to General Grumble, Major Starr had two of his cavalry companies dismounted and staked out on both sides of the Fairfield-Orrtanna road as sharpshooters, in addition to four companies on-mount on the road.[104] With this, they withstood a charge by the 7th Virginia Cavalry. Later this same day, the 6th Virginia Cavalry arrived and felt they could do a better job than the 7th, so they positioned to attack again. According to Edward Longacre, the 6th Virginia was unaccompanied on the second charge and left alone.[30]

This second attack by Elijah's group succeeded in chasing the Union forces for three miles back to Fairfield Gap. They pursued the Union Major Starr's cavalry through Fairfield, where the larger battle ensued with about 400 Union soldiers and 1,050 Confederate soldiers. In the 6th Virginia, three enlisted men were killed, seventeen wounded, five missing; one officer was killed, and two were wounded. They captured 150 Union prisoners. As a result of this interruption, the 6th Cavalry never made it to the battlefield to join General Pickett in the main battle of Gettysburg.[10] At the end of the battle, General Pickett would have no Division left; he had been ordered to cross an open field under heavy fire, which was a terrible mistake and brought hundreds of young men to their early demise.

One of the many joys we had on our adventure was finding treasures, such as this covered bridge, on the road the troops took after they left the Battle of Fairfield. I love driving through these old covered bridges, as the car tires rumbled clackity-clack along the wooden boards of the bridge. One can't help but remember the old Model-T Ford cars and families out on a Sunday drive. As Elijah passed through this area, it is doubtful that he felt as though he was out for a simple Sunday drive. Plus, in July, it would have been very hot and humid, and the stench of men's blood would have filled the air.

Retreating Back to Virginia (July 1863)

On 4 July, the 6th Virginia Cavalry were protecting General Richard S. Ewell, who had replaced General Stonewall Jackson following his untimely death after the battle of Chancellorsville in Guinea Station, Virginia, on 10 May 1863. The wagon train travelled from Gettysburg, through Fairfield, and through Monterrey Pass at South Mountain, which forms the northern seventy-mile extension of the Blue Ridge Mountains through Pennsylvania and Maryland. This is an important geographic landform, as it separates both the Cumberland and Hagerstown Valleys from the Piedmont areas.

In their retreat south, the Confederates continued marching along the road until it met Broad Turnpike, which led to Emmitsburg, Maryland. There was a great deal of confusion and surprise as a Federal battery attacked them, because of the darkness of night and the heavy rains. The 6th Cavalry drew back while firing. This particular storm contained a great deal of lightning, which lit up the area, exposing enemy troops in the blanket of darkness as they retreated and exchanged volleys. On 6 July, as the Federals dissipated, there were a great many wagons destroyed alongside the road. One can only imagine the emotions of each man as they witnessed this destruction.[10]

The balance of the campaign would see the Confederates moving back south to their homeland. It became clear to the Confederates that the idea of an offensive battle had failed. On the 6 July, the retreat led the Cavalry through Ringold and Leithersburg, back to Williamsport, Maryland. The major importance of this particular road they retreated on was that it was the shortest route to and from Gettysburg that crossed the

Potomac. When they came to the Potomac River, they found a partially-swept-away pontoon bridge and extremely high water, which rendered the bridge impossible to cross. Near Funkstown, the 6th Virginia Cavalry was assigned picket duty.[10]

After losing the Battle of Gettysburg, Lee's army retreated through the Fairfield Gap back to Virginia. On 8 July, the march continued south through Boonesboro, and they fought a brief skirmish that forced them to cross at Antietam Creek. On 9 July, as they passed Union Sharpshooters, there was no active engagement.[10] On 13 July, General Lee officially began the withdrawal of his defensive troops on the north side of the Potomac River, Maryland, and later that evening, they successfully crossed the Potomac River and were finally in their beloved Virginia. The troops had to build pontoon trains for troops to cross, but all troops were in Virginia by 14 July.[9] This was a significant movement in the war, as this was the Confederacy's only and final offensive into the Northern territory.

Confederate Troops stayed in Virginia for the remainder of July 1863. The 6th Virginia had been tasked with guarding the Shenandoah River in order to protect General Robert E. Lee's communications between Lee's Army and Winchester. The Shenandoah River was overflowing due to extreme rains that nature had very kindly sent. On 15 July, just south of Charlestown (now in West Virginia), there was a brief volley of gunfire with the Federals; however, no major engagements happened.[10]

Troops were camped at Bunker Hill, Virginia, just north of Winchester and General Lee wrote to Confederate President Jefferson Davis that, "The men are in good health and spirits, but want shoes and clothing badly. As soon as these necessary articles are obtained, we shall be prepared to resume operations."[9] By 24 July, General Lee began moving his Army of Northern Virginia towards the Culpeper Courthouse, which was east of Winchester, Virginia. Elijah and his 6th Virginia Cavalry rode to Front Royal and attempted to cross the Shenandoah River at Chester's Gap, but they found it controlled by the Union. As a result, on 27 July, they decided to ride south to Luray, Virginia, and successfully crossed the river at Thornton's Gap.[10]

Interestingly, this Gap sits between Pass Mountain (north) and Mary's Rock (south). On 28 July, as the group moved west, they set up camp at Culpeper Court House, and on 1 August, the 6th Virginia served as reinforcements to General Wade Hampton's brigade, which had retreated.[10] The counterattack successfully pushed the Union across to the very same field where Generals Stuart and Lee had conducted reviews of the troops at Brandy Station nearly two months earlier.

The Mine Run Campaign Begins (September 1863)

Elijah must have been very tired after all of this riding. On 8 September, according to the Muster Roll taken at the end of August, he was present. At this muster, he also re-ceived payment for cloth-

Kelly's Ford, where both armies crossed the river. Photo by G. Lindner

ing. A few days later, on 13 September, he would soon meet up with the Union soldiers again. At 4 a.m., Union General

Pleasanton advanced from Sulphur Springs toward Confederate General Stuart's headquarters in Culpeper Court House. The Union soldiers attacked at the intersection of Brandy Road and Rixeyville Road before crossing the Rapidan River at Starks Ford and Kelly's Ford.[10]

When we finally found Kelly's Ford, the river was running quite high, with a strong undercurrent. As I stood there, I pondered how in the world could they have crossed this ford, other than to set up temporary pontoon bridges. It was reported that the river was running seven feet high during these battle days. Once again, the 6th Virginia Cavalry was placed on the front line. By 10 a.m., the cavalry was forced back towards Culpeper, through the town and two miles beyond. After taking care of Confederate pickets, they charged the main Confederate position centered at the railroad depot at about 1 p.m. Union Brig. General George Custer led this assault, capturing over 100 prisoners and three guns. The Union Army took the town of Culpeper on this day in the Battle of Culpeper Court House. The Confederates were driven toward the Rapidan River, and they crossed at Raccoon Ford. Here, their position was too strong for the Union Army to capture. On 14 September, the Union Cavalry approached Rapidan Station, as the Confederate artillery continuously fired at them throughout the day. The 6th Virginia crossed the Rapidan to charge dismounted Federal cavalry members that were hiding behind the fence and posts. General J. E. B. Stuart praised Major Flouronoy for his strategies of success and, a few prisoners were taken. Here, 6th Virginia suffered two dead, four wounded, and fifteen taken prisoner.[10]

Remember when Elijah's horse was shot out from under him, and he had to file a claim for reimbursement from the

War Department? Finally, on this day, 18 September 1863, he received compensation for his horse with in a letter from the unit paymaster, which he signed for $350.

There was a great deal of destruction of the beautiful homes and farms that occupied this area, and when the 6th Virginia crossed the Rapidan River, all were extremely upset by the number of farms the Federals had destroyed. Elijah and his cavalry rode through this area towards Barboursville on 22 September to conduct a Federal raid. They were successful, and they drove off the band of Union soldiers. On 23 September, they were able to overcome a rear guard action and continued their march to Orange Court House.[10] At this point, Colonel Julien Harrison from Goochland had been placed in charge of the 6th Virginia Cavalry. On 9 October, General Grumble Jones was transferred to Southwest Virginia and was replaced by Brig-

Orange County Courthouse. Photo by G. Lindner

adier General Lunsford L. Lomax. At this time, General J. E. B. Stuart's Cavalry Corps was reorganized into two divisions under the command of General Wade Hampton and General Fitzhugh Lee. Now, the 6th Virginia Cavalry was placed under General Wade Hampton's command.[10] Union General Buford and his 1st Calvary Division crossed the Rapidan River at Germanna Ford, marched west towards Morton's Ford—another place to cross the Rapidan River. The 6th Virginia Cavalry marched to recapture Morton's Ford. In their quest, they dismounted, charged on foot, and drove the Federals from their breastwork, which was laid down to hold their fire. The Federals barraged them with artillery for an hour, and then their cavalry charged. This failed miserably, and many Federals were killed. As they retreated, the 6th Virginia Cavalry charged, pushing the Federals back across the Rapidan. Another Confederate brigade joined them, and the 6th Virginia Calvary remounted, crossed the river, and joined in the chase.[10]

This was quite a busy day for Elijah, and given that Morton's Ford played an important part in this campaign, I really wanted to stand at Morton's Ford. Unfortunately, Morton's Ford is now on privately-owned property, but during certain Civil War reenactments, the area is opened up in events run by The Friends of the Cedar Mountain Battlefield.

Stevensburg was the next place we found, and there are only a few building in a small clustered area, located on the intersection of Virginia Route 3 and Virginia Route 663. There are also several good wineries nearby, as well as an award-winning distillery, both of which are a staple in Virginia Tourism.

In October of 1863, when the Federals made a stance at Stevensburg, the Confederate cavalry dismounted and opened fire and the Federals fell back to Brandy Station. Next, another Union division showed up on the rear of 6th Virginia, trapping them between two Union Forces. General J. E. B. Stuart approached the rear with his Brigade behind the Union forces and was able to drive off the Union forces that were at the rear of the 6th Virginia Cavalry.[10] On 10 October, the Confederate forces were greatly elated by General Stuart's arrival; thus, the 6th Virginia did a roundabout and attacked the Federal forces behind them in columns of four across. Unfortunately, Colonel Harrison, the leader of 6th Virginia, was severely wounded in his thigh, and Private Opie was also wounded. Next, the cavalry made between seven and nine charges, which all failed. However, they did hold the hill they were on and they battled for nearly three hours. Casualties count was two mortally wounded, fifteen wounded, and several horses killed in action.[10]

General Lee's Confederate Army of Northern Virginia employed nearly the same battle plans and positioned the troops to launch an offensive very similar to troop movements used at the 1862 Second Battle of Manassas, by transporting troops inland, marching towards Manassas, Virginia.[31] On 12 October, they were engaged in skirmished at Gaines' Mills Crossroads, Jeffersonton, Brandy Station, Fleetwood, and Hartwood Church (near Warrenton Springs). That night, they camped at Beverly Ford on the Rappahannock River; the next morning, they crossed the Rappahannock River towards Warrenton Springs, where Union General George G. Meade had his troops encamped. Despite these brief skirmishes, there were no casualties.[10]

These brief skirmishes would continue until Sunday, 18 October, the same day that Elijah's 6th Virginia Cavalry

Catlett Station, Virginia. The site where General J. E. B. Stuart, CSA, and the 6th Virginia Cavalry raided Union Headquarters on 22 April 1862. Photo by G. Lindner

was harassing Union Major Gouverneur Warren's troops.[9] Unfortunately for Elijah, the Confederates did not see the Union Troops, and were ambushed; however, new Confederate reinforcements caused General Warren and his troops to retreat to Centreville. On 19 October, Confederate General J. E. B. Stuart engaged Union General Judson Kilpatrick and his troops at the Battle of Buckland Mills (also known as the Buckland Races or the Battle of Chestnut Hill). Near Buckland Mills on Broad Run in Fauquier County, Confederate General J. E. B Stuart was covering the Confederate retreat from Bristoe Station to the Rappahannock River.[32] Later that day, he turned and charged directly towards the pursuing Federal cavalry, and infantry attacked the flank of the Union cavalry. The Confederates named this skirmish "The Buckland Races", because the pursuit of the Union reminded them of their much-loved traditional Virginia sport of the foxhunt.[32] A few more skirmishes occurred at Catlett's Station, Haymarket, and Gainesville; however, this day would be the last time any fighting of importance would take place in the Bristoe Campaign.[10]

After this indecisive Bristoe Campaign, Union General Meade was being pressured to move his 84,000-man Army of the Potomac across the Rapidan to attack Confederate General Lee's Army of Northern Virginia Army, which was 49,000 strong.[9] The entire Confederate cavalry crossed back across the Rappahannock on 20 October and set up camp. For the next two weeks, Elijah and the 6th Virginia performed picket and scouting duties.[10] This was a very important task, as there were more skirmishes with Union troops at Rappahannock Station, Liberty, and Bealeton, Virginia. 27 October would bring more fighting near Rappahannock Station and Bealeton, Virginia and, a few days later, another skirmish at Catlett's Station, Virginia.

November 1863 came in like a lion while the Confederate Army of Northern Virginia under General Robert E. Lee was encamped along the Rapidan and Rappahannock rivers. This was about to become an explosive battleground between forces. As the 6th Cavalry continued to scout and provide messenger duties between camps, there was a skirmish on 10 November at Falmouth, Virginia.[10] The Union Army of the Potomac under General Meade continued to move forward in their goal, across the Rappahannock River at Rappahannock Station and Kelly's Ford, while engaged in skirmishes along the way. Confederate General Lee withdrew any forces stationed in this area back across the Rapidan River. Fighting broke out in Warrenton, Rixeyville, Jeffersonton, Muddy Creek, Stevensburg, and Brandy Station. Neither army had a moment to breathe, as the action was continuous; they were maneuvering around each other and waiting for any opportunity to win.

As fate would have it, Mother Nature provided Virginia an early snowstorm with very heavy snows, which were certainly not helpful for conducting a successful military campaign. On this very cold and miserable day, 10 November, Elijah and his cavalry crossed between the forks of the Rapidan and the Robinson Rivers.[10] On 11 November, our beloved Elijah was injured in battle. Elijah's service record does not provide details about how he was injured, but given his encounters in battle, more than likely he was shot. It is important to keep in mind that Civil War medicine was very primitive, and antibiotics as we know them today were nonexistent. Fever would set in, and wounds would fester and eventually gangrene if a wound was not tended to. I can't even imagine the pain of being wounded with a mini-ball full of lead. Did Elijah remove the lead bullet himself with a knife to avoid infection? How cold and miserable he must have felt. By 14 November, all the war fronts in Virginia were quiet, and not a shot was heard. One can only imagine the pleasant respite from gunshots and cannons blowing up. Despite this silence, the Civil War was far from being over, and the situation would get much worse for our Elijah as the end of the month rolled around.

Action Along the Rapidan River (November 1863)

On the first officially-celebrated national holiday of Thanksgiving, on 26 November 1863, thousands of families were dearly missing their beloved boys. In the early morning, the campaign front along the Rapidan River began, during which there was quite a bit of fighting. Union General Meade had originally wanted to launch this campaign on 24 November; however, heavy rains hampered this plan. As General Meade with his Army of the Potomac crossed the Rapidan, their goal was to destroy Confederate General Lee's right flank. As the Union crossed, General Meade had hoped to reach Robertson's Tavern on the Orange Turnpike, but because of the heavy Virginia rains, the roads were exceptionally muddy, which slowed the Union forces before they reached their destination.[10]

As dawn broke on 27 November, both sides advanced toward each other. General Lee was waiting south of the Rapidan River, and the Confederates were well entrenched in their positions. The skirmishing began about 11 a.m. near Robertson's Tavern between the Confederate divisions of Major Generals Jubal A. Early and Robert E. Rhodes, along with Union Major General Gouverneur K. Warren's Second Corps. The fighting continued throughout the day, as both sides awaited the arrival of reinforcements. After dark on 27 November, Confederate forces withdrew to prepared field fortifications along Mine Run. Soon after, the Union Army closed in on these positions, and there were heavy skirmishes, but no major attack. The Confederates were able to drive the Federals back across Morton's Ford. The next day, 28 November, brought heavy rains and muddy roads, which hampered the next day's advance. Overnight, the temperature dropped below zero, and without tents, shelters, or even fires, the soldiers shivered through what, for many, was perhaps the worst night of the war. On 2 December, as Confederate troops were very secure in their fortifications, Union General Meade came to the conclusion that an attack was not possible, which ended this winter campaign. As a result, both armies settled into winter camp.[33]

Patriotism had taken its toll on our Elijah Hutchison. He had been captured as a Prisoner of War, had his beloved sorrel mare shot out from under him in battle, and had been shot two times in the last campaign. On 1 December, as Union General Meade gave up his chances of infiltrating the Confederate position, Elijah was reassessing his commitment to war, as he had experienced much more than he bargained for in serving his Virginia.

How much more misery could he take in addition to lack of food, freezing cold temperatures, and two bullet wounds? Service records show that Elijah was injured twice during the Battle of Mine Run, once on 27 November and again on 2 December. Was he shot with mini-balls, and had infection set in? Remember, he had been shot a few weeks earlier, and it is doubtful that he was fully healed from the last wound. That was a hard-fought battle during horrendous rains, snow, and cold. It is possible that Elijah was delirious and wracked with a high fever as the lead from the mini-balls set in for the second time in a month? What was going through his mind as he dodged the mini-ball bullets and cannonballs? The Confederates had no medical supplies, very little food, and no shelter, and they were living in unsanitary conditions surrounded by Union soldiers.

He must have decided that if he were to see his beloved wife and children again, he needed to make a desperate attempt to save himself. It was then that he escaped through Morton's Ford, near Orange County Court House on the Rapidan River—a stream that was four feet deep on the Confederate side. Elijah would have needed to escape via Orange County Court House to make his way homeward; otherwise, he would have gone through the enemy camp. He made the decision to desert the military—a decision which I believe he did not make lightly. Perhaps he felt as though he had given his "country" enough and his time had run out, or perhaps, he felt as though he was at death's door and wanted to see his family one more time. Sadly for us, all these thoughts are lost to history. This decision impacted the rest of his life, as well as the lives of his descendants, because he was labeled as a deserter. This label has followed him throughout the ages, despite the fact that he was in very poor condition and close to death.

Manassas Battlefield or First Battle of Bull Run in Manassas, Virginia. Facing the photograph, the Union Army, under Major General Irwin McDowell, approached the Confederates from the left behind the Yankee canons. Elijah and his 6th Virginia would have been in prone position from the right side, facing towards this scene at the First Battle of Manassas on 21 August 1861. Photo by G. Lindner

CHAPTER 6:
Elijah Returns Home

As he returned from war, we are unsure of where he was from 3 December 1863 until the end of the war. Somehow, he made his way to safety, healed, and must have been home by May 1864 in order to conceive another child with Susan. John Lewis was born on 2 February 1865. We can only imagine the joy and feeling of safety as he arrived home for care from his loving wife, Susan. There is a notation on the July/August 1864 Muster Roll that he was last paid on 31 October 1863 by Captain Carter, and also reflects that he was absent for Muster on 27 December 1863 because of injuries he received on 2 December. The records are certainly not consistent, though, because they list him as deserting on 1 December, despite having received injuries on 2 December. He was also absent on 17 December for Receipt roll and was not paid. The last entry is on 27 December 1864 noting that he was not present for Muster Roll and had deserted.

The War officially ended on 9 April 1865, when General Robert E. Lee, commanding officer of the Army of Northern Virginia, officially surrendered to General Ulysses S. Grant, commander of the Army of the Potomac. After a lengthy siege, he realized it was futile to continue to fight, so he had extensive

Appomattox Surrender. Took place in April 1865, in the parlor of Wilmer McLean's house. Mr. McLean had lived on the outskirts of Manassas, Virginia near Blackburn's Ford when the Confederate Army camped on his property, including General Beauregard and his tent! He moved to the small town of Appomattox, Virginia to get away from the war. Photo by G. Lindner

correspondence with General Grant for terms of surrender. The surrender event took place in a small, rural town in southern Virginia on the main Virginia Railroad Line, at Appomattox Court House, in the parlor of Wilmer and Virginia McLean. The ceremony took place shortly after 1 p.m. and lasted about an hour and a half as each General's staff looked on. 30,000 soldiers were fed and each was given a signed parole, which was a complicated process. Each Confederate soldier was given a pass to return home in exchange for an oath. General Grant and his officers treated each man with respect and dignity as the task was completed. The passes had to be typed on a simple typewriter, signed and delivered, which must have been a massive ordeal for 30,000 soldiers. At General Lee's request and with his gratitude for their service, his men surrendered their arms with the understanding they would return home and not raise arms against the Union again. The very generous General Grant signed parole letters, which were very important, as this allowed the surrendered man to use federal ships and trains, to get food and other supplies from federal stations. Remember, these men were hungry, exhausted, and anxious to return home to their loved ones. Unfortunately, many returned to more devastation and heartache. This event set the stage for the rest of the Confederate Commanding Officers to surrender. On 26 April, General Joe Johnston surrendered to Union General W.T. Sherman in today's Bennett Place State Historical Park, just outside Durham, North Carolina. On 4 May, General Richard Taylor laid down arms at Citronelle, Alabama. On 2 June, General Edmund Kirby Smith, Commander of the Department of the Trans-Mississippi Army, surrendered to Union Major General Edward Canby. On 23 June, General Standhope Watie, Commander of the Confederate Cherokee Indian Forces, surrendered.[34]

Now that the war was over, the South had to rebuild, and so they entered the period known as Reconstruction from 1865 to 1877. According to the 1870 census, Elijah and Susan were living in Dranesville in Fairfax County, Virginia.

An estimated 629,000 men died during our Civil War. The country began to repair the damage. Not only was there massive devastation of the land and buildings, the Southern markets of crops were lost, and many businesses went bankrupt. The once-fertile lands were burned and had to be re-cultivated. Loudoun County had no money to provide any assistance to its residents. This is during the period in America's history when the government did not provide assistance. People who had gold or silver kept it in special reserve, as it was a precious commodity and their Confederate paper money was worthless. Landowners who had been very prosperous before the war

Appomattox Courthouse, Virginia. The well-traveled old road which passes by Appomattox Courthouse, Virginia, where General Robert E. Lee's Army of Northern Virginia surrendered on Palm Sunday, 9 April 1865. Photo by G. Lindner

were penniless. Most of the gristmills, railroads, and bridges had been burned, and livestock had been killed or taken by the Union Army. Farmhouses and fences had been burned, and people had to scrounge for food. The Federal soldiers had looted all the houses in the towns and took what they wanted. Many family heirlooms were lost.

On 16 June 1866, Elijah and Susan would have their last two children, the twins Rodney and Rose; however, Rose was very tiny and only survived a few months. Oral family history has it that Rodney Hutchison remembers his family having a couple of negroes when he was a young child that lived with the family as farmhand; he also remembers a "mammy" that cooked for the family, and the children were not allowed to eat dinner with the parents and adults (from Florence Wilham Moeller). Nowhere in the documented records or census records were there slaves in Elijah and Susan's household. Furthermore, by the time Rodney was born in June 1866, slavery had ended, with the 13th Amendment passed and ratified in 1865.

The 1880 census shows Elijah as head of household, aged 54, married, living in Providence, Fairfax County, Virginia. He was living alone working as a carpenter. Oral family history has it that he and Susan separated sometime during this decade. It is said that Susan was bedridden by this time in her life and had moved with their daughter Lucinda to Dumbarton, S.W., Georgetown, Washington, D.C. Sometime during 1888, their two youngest sons, John and Rodney, moved to Illinois. John had bought forty acres of land and started a farm, while Rodney worked as a farmer in Bald Knob in Logan County, Illinois, as stated in a letter to Rodney's daughter-in-law, Mary L. Scott, dated 2 September 1911. It is believed that Rodney joined John after he had a falling out with his fiancée, Jansey Williams. They took a very handsome photo together at Baker's Photography in Manassas, Virginia.

In 1890, the U.S. City Directory for Washington, D.C. lists Susan Hutchison as head of household, and Elijah is living with her at 2911 Dumbarton Ave, N.W., Washington, D.C. Was Elijah sick, or was he taking care of his beloved Susan, who had been so supportive of him and bore him many children? Susan would pass on 19 May 1897.

Susan had been married almost fifty-two years, and by this time had an enormous number of grandchildren. Her youngest surviving child, Rodney Harmon Hutchison, had just married Emma Althetta Scott on 12 August 1890 in Springfield, Illinois. At the time of mother Susan Ann passing, Rodney and Emma had Frank, born 12 April 1891, and Clarence, born 1 October 1893.

So, what happened to Elijah's many children? It has been difficult piecing together the children's lives after they left home. Here is what we know, according to memories from Elijah's great-granddaughter, Florence Wilham Moeller, in 1975:

- Rodney and his wife, Emma, made a train trip to Washington, D.C. with their youngest daughter Lucie, born 30 October 1907, for a funeral. When his beloved and favorite sister Virginia died, Rodney had received a telegram edged in black. Rodney was so happy to see his brothers and sisters again, and his sister, Susie, wanted to adopt Lucy, as she just thought she was the cutest baby. Susie married Lou Stratton, who worked in the Treasury Department; the pair had no children.

- Mary, Rodney's eldest sister, was a dressmaker in Washington, D.C.; however, I have been unable to locate her in a census, so more digging will be done.

- Margaret, also known as "Maggie," married a man named Mr. Johnson and they had a son, Frank, who was 6'7" tall and became a streetcar conductor—car number Capitol 265. Frank married a German woman, Dora. They lived at 1125 or 1126 Pennsylvania Ave, S.E. in Washington, D.C.

- Virginia Fairfax, who went by "Jennie," married Jim Fearson, who was a Baltimore school custodian in Alexandria, Virginia. Their son, Norman, was 6'8" tall.

After Susan departed this life, Elijah took up residence in Alexandria, Virginia. I wonder if he found employment in this charming, riverside town, as is reflected in the 1900 Census. The Alexandria phonebook records show he was living at 323 Pitt St, and is listed as a Carpenter, head of house, where he lived the remainder of his life. It is sad to think that he lived alone, after he had raised a large family and had been surrounded by loved ones for most of his life. What were his best memories of his life? One can only imagine his thoughts and reminiscences, as he spent those last five lonely years without his beloved Susan. Elijah took his last breath on 13 January 1902. What did he die of?

CHAPTER 7:
Elijah's Final Journey

In trying to pay homage to Elijah several years ago, I did find his grave in Bethel Cemetery, Alexandria, Virginia. My son, Eric (who was only five at that time), and I took photos and we talked about his great-great-great-grandfather, Elijah. In writing *Finding Elijah*, I wanted to share the photo of the two of them together; however, when Eric looked at the photo that was taken in 1987, he noticed that the gravestone was incorrect. We were sitting at the table talking about *Finding Elijah* and I knew that somewhere in my collection of thousands of family photos, I had taken a photo. Where was that photo? I asked Elijah for guidance on finding the photo that was literally buried in a photo album on my shelves, and was led to the photo of Eric by Elijah's grave. I was amazed by the moment with chills, and took the photograph to Eric. We looked at each other and realized that his tombstone has been wrong for 114 years. Eric caught the mistake right off and asked me if I was sure that Elijah was in the cavalry; and then I realized the horror of his headstone being wrong. It seemed to be my destiny to try and correct the mistake that had been made on his headstone. As I began my final journey to try to figure out how I could help Elijah really have peace, I knew it was time to revisit the Bethel Cemetery in Alexandria, Virginia.

On Saturday, 19 March 2016, it was a dreary, cold, and rainy day. I was very excited because it was the first day of spring break and I had planned the entire week around *Finding Elijah*. My sister, Debbie Quast Johnson, and her husband, Gary Johnson, had made the long drive to Virginia to join me for the cemetery visit. As we left the house in the morning, were all were very excited and filled with hope for a successful, interesting adventure. Finally, we arrived at the proper cemetery, after driving around on the very tiny roads through the maze of what I later found out consisted of thirteen cemeteries. The corners on these paths were very tight, and as we made our way through the maze, we were surrounded on all sides by gravestones from all eras of history. I felt chills up and down my spine. There was a Catholic Cemetery, a Jewish Cemetery, a Presbyterian Cemetery, a Free Black Cemetery and many others, which I do not know either the populations buried in each separate cemetery or the specific names of each cemetery. I was looking for Bethel Cemetery, a cemetery privately owned by the Glick Family. The cemetery was full of tiny grass covered ruts that served as roads, were extremely narrow and originally intended for carriages and possibly a 1920 Model-T, but definitely not an F150 truck.

My husband pulled up alongside the road, almost to the Bethel cemetery central road, which I had originally wanted to drive down, but there was a funeral going on. As he parked the car, I jumped out and ran to another cemetery road leaving Debbie, Gary, and my husband in the comfort of the nice, warm, cozy truck. It was so cold, and I felt the rain hitting my lightweight woven coat. Why hadn't I worn a heavier coat? It was 43 degrees, the day before spring officially began. I did not know where to go, so I reached out across the sands of time and

Private Cemetery Elijah is buried in, Bethel Cemetery, Alexandria, Virginia. Photo by G. Lindner

asked guidance from Elijah. It had been twenty-five years since I had found his grave and photographed the stone. I began to feel chills up and down my body as I was led over some very soft graves to his gravesite. Personally, there is something very creepy about walking around in a cemetery, not knowing if you are walking on a grave. Shortly thereafter, not wanting to be left out of a great adventure, my sister Debbie got out of the car as I was almost upon his grave. I had shivers because I was literally being led to his final resting spot through what may have been divine intervention. She was a few seconds behind me, wrapped with a long sweater and scarf. Of course, being from Illinois, she knew how to dress: sweater coat, boots, and a lovely long scarf. She came up next to me and looked at me with her big glasses on. We both just stood there in total shock that we were standing in front of our Elijah's final resting spot. There he was, in his final resting place, and we found ourselves wondering why he was so alone. All of a sudden, we were both engulfed with this moment of terrible sadness for him, because he was estranged from any family members, alone in the cemetery. His tombstone was placed in an estranged spot, with no other relatives around—all alone. At first, we thought it might have been some kind of family plot; however, not one family member was laid to rest next to him for all these years. In a cemetery so large and full of "life," he had quite a bit of well-kept land surrounding his stone, about six empty plots surrounded his gravesite, which was really odd to both of us. Why wasn't he buried next to Susan, his beloved wife, who took care of him until she died? I have been unable to find her grave, so if anyone knows, please send information my way!

The answers to these questions are still waiting to be discovered. Where are his children and his wife buried? Where lies his infant baby Rose, and his young son William? We took our photos, me with my camera, and Debbie with her mobile phone. As we stood there, we pondered his life, his sadness, his service to his country, and the wrong information on the gravestone. Why had no one corrected this after all these years—after all these generations of his children, the last one being our great-grandfather, Rodney? We had many more questions, so we began looking around for someone who could help shed some light on his situation.

Unlike the last time I visited the cemetery, when I could not find anyone, on this particular visit there was more action than I had seen on any of my prior visits. As luck would have it, I spotted someone who looked like he could help us. As I began walking towards the tiny weathered hut, a fine-looking young man came out to greet me. As we became engaged in conversation, I felt very confident that this young man, Kennie, was about to educate me on cemetery life.

Elijah's grave with wrong information on the headstone for his service during the American Civil War. Photo by G. Lindner

I explained to him the problem with Elijah's tombstone and asked him if the owner was around, because I wanted to see what could be done to correct my great-great-grandfather's stone, which was wrong for a few reasons. The first reason was because there were incorrect service dates, and the second being that the marker contains no birth or death dates. According to the Union Citizen's records the 24 year old Elijah Franklin, who served in the Civil War for Captain Lowry, left West Virginia, moved to Missouri and opened a bar establishment with Captain Lowry. After sharing this information with Kennie, he walked us across the cemetery to speak with Mr. James Glick, the owner and operator of the cemetery, who was very nice and quite helpful with information. Apparently, the Daughters of the Confederacy pay for upkeep of the headstones for the Confederate Soldiers, and he believed that the Veteran's Administration had placed the tombstone on the grave.

As Elijah's great-great-granddaughter, I feel as though I have been chosen to correct his stone. However, this is not going to be an easy task because of the prejudices towards Confederate soldiers and bureaucratic rules. This task has already proven to be difficult, even more so because 114 years have passed since the incorrect information was engraved on the government-placed headstone. I went home and sent an email to Mrs. Debbie Mullins, the President of the United Daughters of the Confederacy Martha Custis Lee Chapter, who responded to my email immediately and was quite helpful. However, I was told that since Elijah deserted the cause, they would not recognize him as having served at all. She did tell me that if the UDC historian found out that Elijah had checked into the R.E. Lee camp for Confederate soldiers, then the UDC could accept both Elijah and myself into their organization with full participation; however, there is no record of him in one of these camps.

Next, I contacted the funeral home, wondering who had originally bought the plot and who paid for his funeral, but they don't keep records longer than five years. Dead end, no pun intended! I wanted to know exactly what Elijah died of, so I began searching for his death record. I went to the Department of Vital Statistics and Records in Alexandria, Virginia and was told they don't actually have access to those records, but that I could go online to the Virginia Department of Vital Statistics. I still had a glimmer of hope for the website; however, when I accessed the state website, they only have records dating back to 1915. Why? When I finally reached a live person, after being volleyed around from one menu to another, I spoke with a very nice lady at the Virginia State Library Archives. What she told me was that in an attempt to save money, the General Assembly passed a law that no longer required counties, town, or cities to maintain death certificates from 1896 to 1914. I guess I wasn't really surprised at this finding. His obituary leads me to believe it was old age, but he wasn't really all that old upon his passing. By this point, I had already invested too many hours looking for his Death Certificate, but other than old age, his cause of death is totally lost to the ages.

This is not the end of *Finding Elijah* and setting his record straight. His tombstone must accurately reflect his life, and I will try every avenue I can to get a new stone honoring him and a well-deserved Confederate Cross of Honor on his stone. I understand why he deserted, and the pain and anguish which he lived with for the rest of his life. After the war, all soldiers who asked for a pardon from the United States Government received one; however, the Confederate Government did not give any pardons, and was dissolved at the end of the war. And the ugly fact remains that he deserted his post, and there are no extenuating circumstances that the Daughters of the Confederacy will take into consideration to honor him; moreover, they won't recognize me as having an ancestor who fought for his "country", since he deserted. Rules are rules, no exceptions.

As I searched for more answers on how to actually get a replacement tombstone from the Veteran's Administration, I found out there is indeed an agency that orders markers and replacement markers for veterans' graves from American Wars. After not finding the answer on the government website, I called the National Archives Records Administration and actually spoke with a real person. I was thrilled, thinking that this is definitely going in the right direction. He told me to call Rhonda at the National Cemetery Administration Memorial Programs Service in Nashville, Tennessee.

I spoke with Rhonda, she was very nice and explained the

process, and I explained Elijah's situation: that the tombstone was wrong, and my goal was to correct this governmental error from 114 years ago. Of course, there is always red tape, and I was directed to fill out and fax the VA Form 40-1330 with a color photo of the current tombstone. So I filled out the form, faxed it off, and waited for her email. I was quite impressed with the efficiency of the office, because within one week, I received her email request. Elijah and I, across the dimensions of time, were feeling very hopeful that this was going to happen! The government was going to actually correct the mistake they had made in 1902 concerning the misinformation on the original headstone.

Not! In the next few days, Rhonda sent me an email politely denying my application. She had looked up Elijah F. Hutchison and said the information was correct—that he had served in Captains Lowry's light artillery, and that in 1865 his service record reflects he was twenty-four years old. I re-explained to her that our Elijah was buried there, according to the family history; that the cemetery owner had heard the story; and that Elijah lived a few miles from this cemetery when he died. She was very nice and I sent her our Elijah's obituary from 1902, and she acknowledged the two men were very different in ages. I asked her if she could tell me when the government placed the stone on his grave, and she did not have that information, but she suggested that I call the National Archives and Records Administration to see if they could tell me. Interestingly, that was the organization I had called first. Wow—*déjà vu*!

A few days later, on Friday, the 13th with a full moon, I received the expected denial form letter from the Memorial Programs Service, with a Xeroxed signature on the signature block of the Site Supervisor, Memorial Programs Service. It read,

"We have received your application requesting a Government-furnished headstone or marker for the grave of Elijah Franklin Hutchison […] Because the Veteran died before November 1, 1990, and the grave is currently marked with a headstone or marker in good condition, we are unable to approve your application."

The letter goes on to explain additional reasons for the Veteran's Administration's refusal to replace historic headstones for misinformation, so I conclude that other folks have tried to correct such heinous errors made by the government.

"Discrepancies between information in a soldier's military records and the inscription on a Pre-World War I Government headstone or marker common. In an effort to better preserve national cemetery landscapes in 2004, the National Cemetery Administration updated its Headstone/Marker Replacement Policy to retain all "historic" headstones provided that they are in serviceable condition. The Federal definition of "historic" is 50 years of age or older. For a headstone to be deemed unserviceable, it must be 'weathered to the extent that the name is illegible…or damaged beyond repair.' The policy also limits the replacement of historic headstones in situations when an aspect of the inscription is incorrect. The inscription on the headstone was based on the best information at the time."

I finished reading the denial letter. I guess I hadn't really expected the federal government to provide any help for correction of mistakes made in 1902. President Roosevelt did not create the Veteran's Administration (today's Department of Veteran's Affairs) until summer in 1902, months after Elijah died. So far, I have been unable to find out exactly when Elijah's headstone was placed on his grave.

I have several unanswered questions about the headstone. Where was Elijah's eldest son, Robert Henry, when the stone was placed on his father's grave? Did he ever come to visit the cemetery? None of Elijah's children noticed the misinformation, so who notified the government that Elijah died and was a veteran? His obituary clearly says, "…During the war he was a member of the Sixth Virginia cavalry of the Confederate army and served during the four-years conflict…" Elijah's Record in January 1902 would have been filed in the archives and was available. Furthermore, the obituary was published in the Alexandria Gazette on 13 January 1902. The tombstone information has the service information of a different Elijah F. Hutchison, who was in the Union Army in Captain Lowry's Artillery and he was enlisted in West Virginia in early 1865, at age twenty-four. After the war, this young man moved west to Missouri and opened a bar with Captain Lowry. These documents can be found on Ancestry.com. I am deeply saddened because I will never understand why there was no one to look at Elijah's headstone and contact the agency that placed the stone to correct his service information. Why is there not a birth or death date, or even a loving inscription? Who bought the tiny one-person cemetery plot? All these important details are lost to history, along with Elijah's death certificate. There is no use crying over spilled milk; needless to say, it's time to go on to the next plan for correcting Elijah's headstone information and placing an inscription on his stone.

On a positive note, Friday the 13th brought closure to the hope of getting any help or understanding from Big Brother. Next! Hey, at least I found a Confederate color guard that is willing to conduct the proper burial ceremony in honor of his service that I am fairly confident my beloved Elijah never received.

In this book, I set out to tell Elijah's story; however, throughout this journey, I have realized that I was chosen by him long ago, across the dimensions of time to solve the real problem—his headstone.

Great-Great-Grandfather Elijah Franklin Hutchison,
may you soon rest in peace.

Your story is told, but definitely not over!

WORKS CITED

1. Thomas Jefferson to Martha Jefferson Randolph, Letter, 2 July 1826 (http://tjrs.monticello.org/letter/1558)

2. Wolfe, Brendan. "Unionism in Virginia During the Civil War," Encyclopedia of Virginia During the Civil War. Virginia Encyclopedia in partnership with the Virginia State Library, www.encyclope-diavirginia.org/Unionism_in_Virginia_During_the_Civil_War

3. Loudoun History, Civil War, www.loudounhistory.org/history/Loudoun-cw-divited.com

4. Head, James, Park View Press, *History and Comprehensive Description of Loudoun County*, Virginia, 1908.

5. Lincoln, Abraham. *A House Divided*. Speech. www.abrahamlincolnon-line.org/lincoln/speeches/house.htm

6. *History of the Telegraph, A Few of our Favorite Things: History Wired.* American Museum of History, Smithsonian Institution. www.historywired.si.edu

7. Burke, Davis, Our Incredible Civil War, New York, Rinehart & Winston, 1960, pgs.79-80

8. Selcer, Richard F, Balkin, R, Gen Ed., *Civil War America, 1850-1875, Almanacs of American Life,* Facts on File, New York, 2006.

9. Long, E.B., *The Civil War Day By Day: An Almanac 1861-1865, 1971,* Da Capo Press, New York

10. Musick, Michael P. *6th Virginia Cavalry, The Virginia Regimental Histories Series 2nd Edition.* 1990. H.E. Howard, Inc. ISBN 1-56190-002-8.

11. Battle of Balls Bluff, http://www.civilwar.org/battlefields/ball-sbluff.html

12. Battle of McDowell, National Park Service, US Department of the Interior, 19 July 1995.

13. Newton History Center, Town History, Newton History Center Organization, 5408 Main Street, Stephens City, VA 22655-0143

14. Krick, Robert K. *Conquering the Valley: Stonewall Jackson at Port Republic*. New York: William Morrow & Co., 1996. ISBN 0-688-11282-X, pp. 449, 460

15. Cozzens, Peter. *Shenandoah 1862: Stonewall Jackson's Valley Campaign*. Chapel Hill: University of North Carolina Press, 2008. ISBN 978-0-8078-3200-4. pp. 489–90, 494.

16. Tanner, Robert G. *Stonewall in the Valley: Thomas J. "Stonewall" Jackson's Shenandoah Valley Campaign, Spring 1862*. Garden City, NY: Doubleday, 1976. ISBN 978-0-385-12148-4.

17. "Port Republic." National Park Service, CWSAC Battle Summaries, The American Battlefield Protection Program.

18. Eicher, David J*., The Longest Night: A Military History of the Civil War*. New York: Simon & Schuster, 2001. ISBN 0-684-84944-5

19. Moore, Frank, ed. *The Rebellion Record: A Diary of American Events, with Documents, Narratives, Illustrative Incidents, Poetry Etc., Vol. 6*. New York: G. P. Putnam, 1863.

20. Rowlesburg Area Historical Society Tourist Sign, Rowlesburg Tourism Commission.

21. Jones, Virgil Carrington, "Grey Ghosts and Rebel Raiders." Galahad Books, 1995.

22. *Confederates Capture Fairmont (Virginia), The Battle Of Fairmont: Three Hours Desperate Fighting! 300 Unionists Against 6,000 Rebels.* Fairmont, Va., May 4, 1863, published in the Wheeling Daily Intelligencer, May 5, 1863.

23. McKain, Dave, "Civil War: Burning Springs oil and raids," Parkersburg News and Sentinel, March 1, 2014.

24. Burning Springs, WVirginiaEncyclopedia.org

25. Woodward, Harold R., Jr. "Defender of the Valley, Brigadier General John Daniel Imboden, C.S.A." Rockbridge Publishing Co., 1996.

26. Noirsain, Serge, "40 Millions Dollars in Flames at Burning Springs: The first raid on a petroleum oil site." Translated into English by Gerald Hawkins. Confederate Historical Association of Belgium. http://chabbelgium.com/pdf/english/BurningSprings.pdf

27. "From Brown's Gap to Rockfish Gap." PATC (Potomac Appalachian Trail Club). http://www.patc.us/history/archive/browngap.html

28. Battle of Brandy Station, National Park Service, www.nps.gov/frsp/brandy.com

29. Battle of Upperville, National Park Service, www.cr.nps.hps/abpp/battles/va038.htm

30. Longacre, Edward G. *The Cavalry at Gettysburg*. University of Nebraska Press, 1986, ISBN 0-8032-7941-8

31. Freeman, Douglas S. *Lee's Lieutenants: A Study in Command*. 3 vols. New York: Scribner, 1946. ISBN 0-684-85979-3.

32. Jordan, David M. *Happiness Is Not My Companion: The Life of General G. K. Warren*. Bloomington: Indiana University Press, 2001. ISBN 0-253-33904-9

33. Battle of Mine Run, CWSAC, National Park Service, www.nps.gov/abpp/battles/va044.htm

34. Appomattox Courthouse, National Park Service, www.gov/apco/the-surrender.com

WORKS REFERENCED

Battlefield Appomattox, Civil War Trust, www.civilwar.org/battlefields/appomattox-courthouse.com

Constitution, United States, 1790, https://www.law.cornell.edu/constitution

Loosbrock, Richard D. "Battle of Brandy Station." *Encyclopedia of the American Civil War: A Political, Social, and Military History*, edited by David S. Heidler and Jeanne T. Heidler. New York: W. W. Norton & Company, 2000. ISBN 0-393-04758-X.

"Manassas Station Operations." CWSAC Battle Summaries, The American Battlefield Protection Program.

"Myth: General Ulysses S. Grant stopped the prisoner exchange, and is thus responsible for all of the suffering in Civil War prisons on both sides." http://www.nps.gov/ande/learn/historyculture/grant-and-the-prisoner-exchange.htm

O'Neill, Robert F. *The Cavalry Battles of Aldie, Middleburg and Upperville: Small But Important Riots, June 10–27, 1863.* Lynchburg, VA: H.E. Howard, 1993. ISBN 1-56190-052-4.

"Potomac River During the Civil War." Virginia Encyclopedia in partnership with the Virginia State Library. www.virginiaencyclopedia.org /Potomac_River_During The_Civil_War

"Slavery in Virginia, A Map." www.virginiamemory.com/online_classroom/shaping_the_constitution/doc/slavemap

The War of the Rebellion: a Compilation of the Official Records of the Union and Confederate Armies, U.S. War Department, U.S. Government Printing Office, 1880–1901, Series I, Vol. XXIX, Part 1, p. 9.

Geneva Lindner, M.Ed., M.A. History

Geneva grew up in the prairie state of Illinois, affectionately known as "the Land of Lincoln." Living on the outskirts of Peoria, she attended Dunlap High School, and later joined the United States Navy as a photographer. She earned her under-graduate degree and two graduate degrees from George Mason Uni-  versity. She has been teaching high school American History for nearly twenty years, and has taught American History at Northern Virginia Community College. Her love of nature and adventure, along with a passion for family genealogy, led her to embark upon a journey to follow her great-great grandfather Elijah F. Hutchison's adventure in Civil War Virginia. Geneva currently resides in Clifton, Virginia with her husband and an assortment of four-legged fur babies. Completion of her book, *Finding Elijah,* is the culmination of a tribute to Elijah and all extended family members, as well as those beloved ancestors who rest with the Angels.